How to be your own Saving Grace

15 steps to happiness, joy and peace

ANNA WILLE

For my dream team Nina, Oskar and Lara.
Thank you for choosing me and for being by my side on this
mostly wonderful journey.
May you always feel loved and loveable.
You can choose to do anything with your lives, but remember
to choose happiness.

For Mum.
May you find freedom from pain and release the hurt.
You don't need to be strong and fiercely independent anymore.
Surrender.
You are not alone.

For anyone who has fallen and is finding it hard to get up.
Start with you and everything will fall into place.

HOW TO BE YOUR OWN
Saving Grace

Fifteen steps to find Happiness, Joy and Peace
by learning to:
Love Yourself
Live in this moment
Lead the life you desire.

BY
Anna Wille

saving grace

noun:

1.   the redeeming grace of God.

           "the sudden intervention of God's saving grace"

2.   a redeeming quality or characteristic.

           redeeming feature, compensating feature, good point,
           thing in its favour, thing in one's favour, appealing aspect,
           attractive aspect, advantage, asset, selling point

How To Be Your Own SAVING GRACE

INTRODUCTION

Sometimes events in our lives knock us down. They take us by surprise and wind us, leave us sitting on the floor in despair. Whether it's the end of a relationship, losing your job or falling ill, we have two choices; stay down and let life pass us by, or get up, get sorted, and live a life we never even dreamed of.

But that can be hard to do and sometimes we simply don't know where to start, how to get up? Or we have no one reaching out a helping hand to lift us up. The good news is you don't need anyone to lift you up; you can do it by yourself. You just need to know how.

This book offers a way to start your journey ... to help you to get up off the floor ... to be your own SAVING GRACE. The many varied and often bonkers steps explored may not all tickle your fancy at first glance, but one thing is certain, they make the journey colourful and the results proved to be better than expected.

Keep an open mind; you don't know until you've tried ... and if nothing else, keep trying, until you are standing so tall, that the floor is completely out of sight. Oh, and remember to have FUN!

Through this journey you'll see that, like weebles, people wobble, but we don't fall down, at least we don't STAY down. Like the phoenix, we can rise from the ashes of our broken heart, broken bank account or broken body stronger, brighter, and happier than we ever imagined. You just have to breathe in ... and get up.

You've taken the first step by deciding to help yourself, by buying this book and by opening the cover ... so now, just keep going. On, On! See you at the top!

BACKGROUND – WHY THIS 'GRACE'* NEEDED SAVING

(*Anna comes from the Jewish name Hannah, meaning Grace - something I sometimes lost in my struggle to stay strong, and something I attempt daily to embody. Sometimes successfully!)

How do I know what it feels like to be alone, broken or ill? What gives me the right to tell you what to do to get up off the floor? My fall wasn't the first of its kind and sadly won't be the last. But it might resonate with you, it might help you understand that you are not alone, that it isn't a question of who is to blame or why you? It will show you that even from a hard, lonely place on the floor, you CAN get up and live. Live happily, joyously and beyond your wildest dreams.

2010. Things had been dodgy for a while. Well not things, him. Us. And maybe not dodgy, just distant ... in words, not space. Completely silent at times. But then I'd been led to believe that that was normal, after three kids and 18 years together. Then one day, totally unexpectedly, my world imploded and I found myself crumpled on the kitchen floor in SW London, unable to get up. Unable to do anything. Except cry.

My wobble was definitely high magnitude on the Richter scale. In the space of just one word, I went from being a recently re-patriated co-parent of 3 beautiful children aged three to nine, about to embark on another exciting phase of married life ... to a single parent, whose husband had decided, without any consultation or warning, to live 1400 miles away ... indefinitely. In other words - words he was unable to utter for another 4 years - to slowly end our marriage. Not because he's a bad person – simply because, like all of us, that's all he could do with the emotional intelligence coping skills he had at the time. I know that now, but at that moment it felt like abandonment and betrayal.

Anyway, despite wanting to just curl up and hide, my newfound single-parent situation meant that I had to get my shit together or things would fall apart. So, for three years, parts of my life were 'business as usual' on the surface, while below the veneer, I tried to make sense of my new place in the world, tried to find out who I was, incessantly searching for answers but only finding more questions.

And the biggest one of them all: Why me?

And as I look back now in my new mindful, grounded wisdom, I realise that for those three and a half long, hard years of our initial separation, I pretty much committed each of the seven 'sins' of Mindfulness:

- I judged others and myself, compared myself to others who had managed to stay 'together' and blamed myself for everything about my new situation
- I was impatient, wanting things to get fixed quickly
- I was in constant disagreement and disbelief about a different way ahead, rather than have a beginner's mind about the future, a curiosity to start afresh
- I lived on high-alert survival mode, doubting things

would work themselves out without extreme effort and trusting nothing to unfold naturally, least of all a good outcome

- I strived like a bull before a red rag, trying to get things done my way, to my schedule
- I rejected my new situation, refusing to accept things as they were, and instead just wondered why? Why? WHY!?!
- Worst of all I was attached, as if with super-glue, to life as I had known it until then. I just wouldn't let go; like a dog with a bone I was determined to get my old life back, whether it served me or not. I turned my back to the new door in front of me, unaware of the endless opportunities on the other side, refusing to even hold the handle and just kept going back through old doors, time and time again. Getting nowhere.

Then, just when I had found a numb and monotonous but manageable place to exist from, still insisting on trying to make things work, albeit with less energy and enthusiasm, I was knocked down yet again. The revelation that a new love had taken my place winded me once more, but it packed a much mightier punch. The floor became my home again. The tears returned and this time they stayed for four months, relentlessly reducing me to unashamed, unhidden sobbing.

If any of the above sounds familiar … the good news is, it means you're human. These are the actions of a person who's hurt, sad, worried and scared. Not mean, stubborn or crazy. Just broken. And as Leonard Cohen said

"There is a crack in everything, that's how the light gets in".

But when your vision is blurred by salty tears, it's hard to see the light. This book aims to guide you to it, however dim and distant it might seem; to offer you ways of looking at the world more softly and grabbing life by the horns with greater confidence, so that you can save yourself from endless tears or numbness. The suggestions will lift you up, fill you with self-love and enable you to live a life filled with joy, happiness and peace. Some of the journey can feel sad, as we learn to let go, some of it is hilarious, as we experiment with a beginner's curious mind, and ALL of it is transformative.

The fifteen steps in this journey will let that light in, ray by ray. They offer a lightly spiritual journey of self-discovery, from herbal spirit-cleansing to bio-energetic dance, in a quest to understand how life unfolds (sometimes painfully) as it does. Until one day, without striving, you will realise, as I did, that you don't need to find or see the light .... you ARE the light. So now may the light I found in me, shine in you, whether you are a woman or a man, 30 or 60. If you have come to a place in life where it's hard to get up and believe in yourself, in love, may this help you RISE up and SHINE.

PROLOGUE – THE IMPORTANCE OF GETTING TO KNOW WHAT YOU DON'T KNOW

Before taking the first step on the path to happiness, there are a few questions worth asking yourself. I have been inspired by many wise spiritualists, coaches and authors over the last seven years. The seeds for some of the questions below have been planted in me by reading and watching the work of

Marisa Peer, best-selling author, motivational speaker, Rapid Transformation Therapist and hypnotherapist, who has helped me and thousands of others understand that 'I am enough'.

The big question: why are you thinking, saying and doing the things you are? Our subconscious isn't as 'sub' as you'd think. Get to know you. What you will find out will change your life.

As we drift through life on auto-pilot, not questioning anything while life is sweet, not listening to those little gut instincts that pop up once in a while, there might be something hiding in our subconscious, driving our thoughts, words and actions, sometimes unhelpfully. Unless we check in with who we truly are, how happy we truly are, what we truly value and how we truly want to live our life, we can find ourselves living a lie, never being the best, happiest version of ourselves. When we aren't true to ourselves, we end up living in a way that limits our growth and abundance, and sends us in directions that aren't aligned with our true path. Sometimes we need to be derailed, to get on the right track.

Question 1: Were you happy as a child?

For example, if you were to ask me whether I had a happy childhood, I wouldn't hesitate to say yes. Despite losing my father to depression and suicide when I was two (the horrid truth about which was kept from me until it was hurled at me when I was seventeen), living in a council flat where the communal entrance was constantly used as a toilet, and being babysat every night, so my mother could work nights to pay the rent, I only remember the good bits. Even at an early age, my subconscious-self buried each unpleasantness – the dead dad, the stinky stairs and the absent mother. I ignored all that. But hiding from sadness does not make it go away. Instead it becomes a latent block to future happiness, as we subconsciously begin to gather false beliefs about how life is. In my case; that people will leave us, nice homes will be hard to come by and parents don't have time to care for or love us …

Until we are forced to get to know ourselves by breaking down, our mind cleverly (but short-sightedly) focusses on the happy memories. For example, driving home in the late 70's, joyously jumping around in the boot of the teal two-door VW estate, not a seat belt in sight, I ignored all the sad bits. I thought it was normal to explore the stale kitchens of the restaurants my mother worked in, where the closed sign hung on the door to the outside, but the wine was very much open inside. And it was fun watching Fred the blue budgie fly around the L-shaped lounge of our tiny council flat, after my brother and I 'accidentally' left the cage open, while our mother's sleeping eyes were shut. Or watching Noel Edmunds' Swap Shop under a duvet den, sharing a box of Sugar Puffs, while Mum was asleep having got home from work at 3am. It was all normal. It was all OK. I never questioned it. At least not consciously.

I didn't question whether there existed a different, let alone better, way of being brought up. I saw the good in what I had. Which is just as well, as in hindsight there was plenty I didn't have. But now I realise that, even though I didn't begrudge a lack of a father or a house with clean stairs or bedtime stories, seeds were planted in those early years that would grow into forests of doubt, fear and yearning, which would, in part, drive my actions later on in life and would affect how I dealt, or failed to deal effectively, with the rocky bits and eventually the end of my marriage. So at some point we all need to befriend our forests of unknown fears, if we are to take control. The only way to trust that abundance – of love, money or health - will come, is to know where your fears and doubts that block this abundance lie. And the only way to know that, is to look in the mirror and ask yourself.

My mirror moment didn't come until I was 40. Until then as a child, it was normal to say goodnight to my mother on the phone every evening. It was normal to battle my way home against the wave of spiteful pupils from the comprehensive opposite my home, out of which stories of knife-wielding and shagging in the stationary cupboard emanated. It was normal (but felt unfair) to be pushed in the way of the 85 bus, just for wearing a purple private school uniform, having been lucky enough to get one of the last 'assisted places' abolished by Maggie.

As I didn't feel sad, I didn't feel the need to 'get happy'. On the surface I thought I was happy, but looking back now, it is so obvious that I was just RESIGNED. I wasn't joyous. I accepted my lot, without wanting or asking the universe for more. And funnily enough people would just say I was calm, collected and mature, never questioning why I wasn't over-excited, exuberant and loud, like a happy child should be ... This just shows how important it is to look below the surface of your happiness as a young adult or even a teen, so that we don't unknowingly drag latent unhappiness into our later life.

***Question 2: Are your values yours, or do they come from
what you have absorbed from your parents and teachers?***

My prize-winning A-Level results at a top London girls' school
hinted at potential for a promising future with an Oxford
degree in languages. So my teachers, genuinely believing I was
Oxbridge material, sent me off to have a look. Never asking
me what I wanted, they tried to propel me into a world of
academic intellectuals, who thrived off literary questioning and
philosophising. But it wasn't meant for me; I felt no connection
with the place or people and spent the morning of the interview
at Christ College perfecting my blusher rather than my Brecht.
For security, I held on to the 'safe' idea of following in my family's
lesser footsteps.

I couldn't explain why at the time, but the dark, imposing
buildings at Oxford felt cold and alien. Even though I loved
speaking the languages I had learnt and would study, and
enjoyed most of the books we were set, the traditional path of
a language degree didn't spark anything in me. I valued being
able to communicate with people and experience their cultures
in their words. I even enjoyed most of the stories (especially the
ones about human relationships and vulnerability: Candide, All
Quiet on the Western Front, Stories from the Viennese Forest,
Zanzibar or The Last Reason ...). I felt urges to learn more and
begged to be allowed to take on Italian A Level, but was denied
the chance by teachers who said I would mix them all up if I
learnt a fifth language. They feared the consequences rather than

trusted my instincts. Already then I was taught to supress my natural inclinations … and to follow a safer, traditional path. So having failed to get into Oxford, just after my 19th Birthday, off I went to Bristol Uni to study French and German. Today my 'job' involves talking to people all day about a different kind of literature, emotional literacy. I still want to learn Italian (having visited it Naples, the Amalfi Coast and Rome twice in the last four years). In fact, I now want to learn Swahili too. I have re-found my passions and values. And this time they are truly all mine.

Question 3: What do you do when the unknown scares you off? Do you embrace your decisions, reassuring yourself you are right, without ever stopping to reconsider?

Like many 'middle-class-educated' teens in the late 80's, I set off down the M4 in my orange VW Golf, with my Jigsaw jeans, black wraparound top and leather Filofax, camouflaged in my safe 'uniform'. Languages were easy for me, so I spent four years surrounded by my future banker, lawyer and doctor friends, who failed to influence my dream of becoming a mere Hotel General Manager. If anything, those years fired the embers of that Hotel Career dream, providing me with the perfect bellows – a year in France and Germany to perfect my languages, as I worked in 5-star hotels. They were filled with bed-swapping cabin crew of the 'flying geese' brigade and red-carpeted A-list movie celebs, hoping for a golden palm, while wannabees paraded their breasts along the Croisette, hoping to be 'talent' spotted. I took everything in and questioned nothing. It was fun, so my choices were ratified. I knew nothing about the worlds of banking or law and so never questioned whether there was more available to me than what I had grown up with ... Being exposed to and aware of all the opportunities out there, ensures we can consider all the options and choose our path from a place of knowledge and confidence, avoiding digressions from our purpose, even if we don't know it yet.

Question 4: How does the goal for 'happiness' fall off your radar?

We are all born wanting to be happy. Wanting food, warmth, safety and human contact. And love. Recognition by, and time with, those we love. And most of all we want to feel self-esteem and to achieve our full potential. That, as beautifully explained by Maslow, is a human's aim. But sometimes, even by a very young age, we lose sight of that and settle for less.

Personally, at the age of 22 my idea of happiness was to be a Hotel General Manger (or GM as they are known; genetically modified to care about bums on beds, yield, and customer satisfaction scores). This was no surprise, having spent my life surrounded by waiters, chefs and restaurant managers, most of them expats who'd fled Portugal's dictatorship in the 60's for the greener pastures of Carnaby Street and Cheyne Walk. My upbringing and environment hadn't suggested searching for self-esteem or self-actualisation and so influenced my choice of 'goal'. I didn't question it. Even my 'posh' private education could only influence me so much. Catering was in my blood (or so I thought); I had been conceived above my parents' Bottleneck Bistro in

Barnet and this apple wasn't falling far from the tree. Rather than experience joy and happiness, my young eyes had seen darkness, hardship and toil, which became my subconscious frame of reference before I was even three, so I set off on a path I believed to be mine, unaware of the loftier heights of happiness available. Rather than settle for satisfaction, it is important that we realise that happiness is something we all deserve and should work towards.

Question 5: Does it work to drift through life, skimming the surface of why you are here? What you value, what is important to you, what makes you feel ALIVE? Or do we need to dive deeper to find meaning and purpose?

During those four years of going with the flow at Uni, I made fabulous life-long friends and found my future husband, but I also found out I didn't value or enjoy knowledge of French or German history or linguistics (ironically the latter is now a passion, so perhaps it was just a question of poor teaching or timing?). Most lectures and tutorials had felt awkward and foreign. I drove back down the M4, with amazing memories but a relatively poor excuse for a degree in hand (yes, I know, I am judging myself here). Looking back to what I knew had previously given me a buzz, without hesitation, I promptly enrolled in a Hotel Management course and embarked on what I thought was the career of my dreams. I didn't ask myself why it was my dream. I just wanted to do something I enjoyed and knew. Something safe. I didn't dig deep to understand why; purpose never came into it. Whether you get there by digging deep, or just by sitting still and letting the truth float to the surface, in order to feel at one with your path, it is key to find that meaning and purpose.

Question 6: Does 'safe' work?

For a while everything seemed to be going as planned. This time I was doing a course I had chosen, not my teachers. I was living with a young man I totally loved and I was learning real life skills – profit and loss sheets, how to fill a rota, how to tell a good wine from a poor one. The daily commute to Victoria felt very grown up after the student-filled stroll to Clifton. And the diversity of the small group of people on my course offered a closeness that I hadn't felt in the huge languages department at Bristol, where uber-academic tutors held lessons in wood-panelled rooms, to discuss authors whose profoundness escaped me. After twelve quick months I graduated with a qualification I could be proud of and soon found work in a prestigious hotel on Hyde Park Corner. The plan was going well indeed. I had a newfound spring in my step and felt happier than ever.

Then, despite rapid promotions, the shine began to wear off. After four years earning less than my savvy Bristol peers, reality bit. Yes, the staff were great (and the staff parties greater). Yes, the food was free. But the pay was … painful. As my city-working friends showed the power of their pay-slips with Paul Smith and Pol Roger, I became aware that mine pulled a less powerful punch. I began to judge my lower income and myself as lesser than. Doubt crept in and undermined what I thought were strong foundations in my passion for Hotel Management. And so, a new ambition was born. Having never been driven by money, I sold my soul to the devil that doubled my salary. I left the safety of where I felt at home, determined to give the establishment a go, but feeling totally out of my depth. Insecurity and imposter-sensations began to develop. Did I belong here? And although some good can happen once we step out of our safe comfort zone, true magic requires us to get way out into the unknown.

Question 7: Does acting through fear, not love, work?

Nevertheless, working in a Big 4 accountants' and consultancy Firm in Aldwych, awash with the cream of the crop of England's finest Uni's, drive, ambition and progression soon changed in me, from overwhelmed, to overpaid and underprepared for what lay ahead. Before I knew it, I was attached to my Samsung wheelie-case and eating dry roasted cashews in the BA First Class lounge, flying to meetings in three countries in one day, gathering mini shampoo bottles as I went. Work no longer involved training illiterate chamber maids to speak English, or teaching friendly Antipodeans customer service to please grumpy Americans. Now, in 1999, the dot.com bubble was growing exponentially, as were my Airmiles, as I was hand-picked to lead a project to upskill 10,000 staff for the needs of the New Millennium. I barely had time to take in how far I had come, from the windowless basement office in Portman Square five years earlier, to beside the EMEIA Managing Partner's corner office over looking the Thames at Temple, where I prayed that I wouldn't be chastised for missing a formula on a spreadsheet, or misunderstand the skill-set of SAP programmers.

Despite living on the edge of my seat, barely believing I had what it took, I had fun drinking the holy water, as it flowed generously from bottles in the Champagne bar below and ignored the slight undercurrent of unease. My work felt every bit as successful as my friends' in their banks and law firms ... but it didn't feel 'mine'. For us to be in alignment, we have to pursue jobs or work that come from a place of truly loving what we do, not a fear of missing out.

Question 8: How do you deal with change?

Riding the wave of my rapid success, I was not at all prepared for what was to follow. A titillating move with The Firm to South America as a newly-wed, opened up worlds I had never seen. My Samsung continued to wear away its wheels in the much more exotic airport lounges of Buenos Aires, Sao Paulo and Santiago. Although I was blissfully happily married, building a home near the Bosques de Palermo and with a baby in my tummy ... I soon began to hate my job. I compared my new lovely but less-worldly colleagues and my new antiquated offices (life in BA in the 80's and 90's had been hard), to my previous upbeat peers and swanky, modern surroundings ... and judged. There was little curiosity in me, just growing frustration at everything being so 'inadequate'. I craved after what I had left behind. I didn't want to let go of the old and accept the new. So, for a year, I made up for that dissatisfaction by exploring the five corners of Argentina; from the lofty plateaux of Jujuy, to frozen glaciers of Ushuaia, from the roaring falls of Iguacu, to the white waters of the Andes and whale-watching cliffs of the Valdes Peninsula. Unable to lean into the 'flaws' of my work environment with a beginner's mind, my bitterness towards my job was growing, but luckily so was my love for the country, and so harmony was mostly maintained.

Then, shortly after the twin towers fell and our binary baby was born (on 01.10.01), a certain oil giant collapsed, exposing and indeed destroying, the Firm and 80,000 jobs with it. Before Christmas an entire South American country tango-ed itself away from the dollar, and after just 15 months in beautiful Buenos Aires, I was forced to return to the UK ... married, jobless and breast-feeding. We had planned five to ten years of South American adventures, but as I know now, the universe laughs in the face of plans ... And I had been so busy moving away and back again, that I hadn't stopped to acknowledge how I had responded to all the changes in my life. We might believe we are adaptable and adapting, but often we just aren't recognising an urge to control things or a desire for things to be different.

Question 9: How resilient are you? Or are you just keeping busy?

Have you ever noticed how when push comes to shove, what works is stopping the self-pity and just getting on with things? Leaving the saucepan revolution and barricaded motorways behind (and a $2000 dollar loss), I felt a new wave of energy, as we were greeted by snowy streets in SW6. Despite the fall in temperature and in luck, I stood defiant in the face of adversity;

bills, nappies and a depressed, jobless husband failed to knock me down. I had a sense of purpose – to set up a new house and start again … again. Even four months alone in London with a six-month old baby, while hubby worked in Bangladesh, didn't rock me. I was just pleased to be in a land I understood and felt at one with. However, by the time baby was nearly one, despite entertaining my grey cells with a course in Interior Design, the feeling of purposefulness was diminishing, and after a year on just one salary, so were our savings.

Did I stop to ask myself what was important and what did I value before taking the next step? The hell I did! I just charged ahead, re-mortgaged the flat, sent out CVs and re-mortgaged my soul to the devil of all devils; I entered the world of banking. Having never understood nor admired the world or money-making, I found myself pushing through the revolving doors not just of the Bank but of life itself. Striving. I see now that sometimes a change of scenario keeps us busy enough to ignore how vulnerable we feel below the surface.

Question 10: How many mistakes does it take to figure out your approach stinks?

Luckily, I had a soft landing, as Dutch banks are much less aggressive than American ones (or so I am told). Even so, working with people whose goal it is to be the youngest person in the building to own a Ferrari, makes it quite easy to realise you've made a BIG mistake. Not even the reduced hours nor the salary that had tripled in five years, were compensation enough for the sensation that my soul was actually being sucked out of me as I placed my electronic entrance card on the shiny steel gates, which opened to let me in, leaving humanity behind me. Despite meeting some great people, who rebalanced my preconceptions of what bankers are like, my money-seeking ambition died. The disconnect between where I was working and what I valued, grew too wide. The misalignment with my values, devalued the large sums of money I received at the end of every month. After just twelve months, a new path to happiness was sought. As my own interior felt toxic in the world of wholesale banking, I turned my efforts to what I really loved at the time and started a business in the world of others' interiors. This might seem just as superficial – dealing with fabrics and furniture – but helping others fall in love with their homes made me HAPPY. What wasn't obvious at the time though, was that yet again I had brought change into my work life, subconsciously hoping that it would make things better in my love life.

Question 11: Do you fall out of love with a person or with life?

For the next four years I was happy. Forget the three R's of my privileged education; this was the age of the three P's, as I pottered between projects, pregnancies and properties, with no other goal than to spend time doing what I wanted, when I wanted, for whom I wanted. The projects got bigger, the pregnancies too. In my second I looked like I'd swallowed a basketball, like St Exupery's snake with an elephant inside it (today at seventeen years old he's six foot two, so that explains that!). Before I knew it, I was managing refurbishments worth a quarter of a million pounds, and much more in love with form and function, and materials and colours, than rude clients, who had more cash than kindness.

And so yet again reality kicked in. Our home got bigger, as did the mortgage. But the time spent with the father of my children got smaller. I had endured the first Dhaka separation easily, distracted by the joys of motherhood. The second, longer stint alone with Thing 1 was harder, as I worked full time and was popping with Thing 2. There were some blissful times when Thing 2 was born, which seemed to bring us closer. But by the time Thing 3 came along, both job satisfaction and time together were practically non-existent. Date nights became evenings alone on the sofa with baby, watching Trinny and Susanna style someone whose figure was much more shapely than my post-baby one. And weekends became tense, as Saturday mornings started around a man asleep on the sofa after a late night (or early morning) out. Things came to a head one day, when we crossed paths, as I buggied the kids to school, which was what got me out of bed each day, as he got home from drinking, which had become what helped him ignore work problems each month and kept him out of our bed … The friend in me wanted to hug him and hear his troubles (which he never shared), but the neglected and hurt wife and mother just gave him the cold shoulder or shared bitter criticisms. Our love was concealed behind the sharp edges of life with three kids under six. On the surface of so many relationships it can appear as if people have simply drifted apart, but often we are unhappy with our careers or selves. Falling out of love with life can be even scarier than falling out of love with a person. The latter often seems easier to change …

Question 12: Why do we seek change, expecting it to stop us being unhappy?

As we stood like strangers at the cliff edge of our marriage, living each day but not ALIVE, the wheel of fortune suddenly seemed to turn favourably. An opportunity to start afresh abroad arose again. My lifelong dream to live in Portugal again became a possibility. A home by the sea, a stone's throw from the stunning city of Lisbon, felt like a welcome change – a return to a place we had enjoyed extensively as a young couple before kids would surely refresh us and remind us of our love and fun times together? In no time at all we found schools for the kids, tenants for our SW18 house and were off! Well at least the kids (aged 6 months, 3 and 6 years) and I were off, as an advance party until his new job started. Tense and exhausted after packing up the house and living at mums for a month, and suddenly filled with insecurity and doubt, that happy vision faltered. As we parted temporarily at the airport, I warned (unknowingly accurately) that our unresolved issues would rear their ugly heads one day unless something between us, not our place of residence, changed ...

Nevertheless, we were hopeful that a new location would inject new breath into our lives. Our London problems were buried. We enjoyed the sea, sand and sunshine. We made new friends and strengthened bonds with my family. We bought a house and enjoyed a slower pace of life, where his job satisfaction was finally back up there. However, those three years in Portugal were transactional, not transformational. Despite his exotic workplace and my seaside school run, there was little difference to OUR happiness; I continued to get up, get the kids to school, try and fail to start a business, collect the kids, dinner, bath, stories and bed. Sure, we made good, lasting friends with expats at the kids' school and we saw my family once in a while. Time just rolled forward. And in the absence of any meaningful communication or soul-searching, we continued to roll apart. Then, persistent as it is, the universe dealt us another blow, in the shape of the Portuguese recession triggered by the US housing crash. Increases in school fees and decreases in salaries. What I see now as one of several opportunities to take stock, re-evaluate, remind ourselves of what we held dear to us, and go back to why we fell in love and follow a path to happiness ... tipped us over the edge. We were just too tired from three babies and three international moves. Too depressed. We didn't have the energy or skills to remember love, to do anything other than fall apart ... And often when couples fall apart they expect that to make things better, unaware of a sadness within our relationship with ourselves, that won't be resolved by a change of relationship with others.

Question 13: Why don't we stop to remember what it felt like when we were happy?

After the wettest winter in Portugal, with one hundred and twenty days of rain falling from the skies, disappointment had spread into every nook and cranny of our relationship. By the time we had conceded defeat, packed up the house and flown back to the UK, we were two bodies living in a house with three children. But we WERE together. And that's all that mattered to ME. We just needed to sort things out, I thought. Find ourselves again. It warmed me that in all that sadness and sense of failure, I still wanted to fix things, to keep our family together. To hold onto love. Amidst all the brown boxes, worn with life, I finally began to realise what was important. Not the job. Not the location. Just happiness. Just love. And true to my name, I was convinced that where there is a Wille, there is a way.

But it takes two and only one of us was in that place. Six weeks after returning to the UK alone, my doubt and insecurity were unbearable; I needed to know when he would be joining us. The morning after our joint 40th birthday party, unable to bear any longer his inability to commit to a return date, unable to endure not knowing how much longer I would be living alone with three kids, with fortnightly visits from their dad, and not a phone call in between, I cornered him, literally. There, back up against the kitchen cupboards, after an eternity of silence in the face of my barrage of an inquisition, he finally got the words out; he wasn't coming back. He didn't want to walk away from his Portuguese project. What about OUR project, I yelled? Our family? I told him I didn't want THIS, get out. So he walked out.

Once alone, I crumbled. One by one, the petals of my fragile soul fell and I sat on the kitchen floor, and cried. I cried every tear in my incredulous body. And the tears ran for four months. What struck me months later was that, in those four years of tension, not once did we have a calm, heartfelt discussion about why we had got together in the first place; what we liked about each other, the passions we shared, the dreams we both had. So often

23

couples fall apart focussed on how they feel in the moment, only paying attention to raw emotions that have arisen from recent struggles and stresses, provoking their survival instincts. When we calm our heartbeat down however, that fear subsides, and (if it is still there) the love that was there in earlier years can whisper to us and bring clarity to why we are unhappy, so that we can deal with the real cause of our unhappiness, and not just the symptoms.

Question 14: How the f**k do you get up from that?

That was over eleven years ago. I have been a new woman for a long while now, literally, as they say your cells regenerate every seven years! I know now what I didn't know then about myself. The path back to full bloom was long and hard, as I slowly uncovered answers to the questions above, but I feel like the prize flower at Chelsea Garden show. How? It all started with a book on a shelf in a holiday home and went on through the many steps in this book below. Finding that book and exploring many avenues, showed me that, however painful it seems at the time, we are all in exactly the place we should be right now – things happen for a reason. I hope that finding this book, will help start or reboot your journey too.

With courage, patience, self-compassion
(and a few friends), in time we
can all learn to see that we are the light we need.

No one can take that away from us. No matter how much shitty water life throws on our fire. No matter how dimly the embers glow. We are all a phoenix waiting to rise. But as we rise, we do so as part of a greater thing. Seven billion people on this planet alone. Who knows how many others out there. That's a whole lot of energy in our universe. That energy helps us rise. It props us up when we feel alone. My aim is that some of my energy can find you in the pages of this book. Take it. Soak it in. Let it relight your fire. It's yours to keep until you are ready to pass it on to someone in need.

So, ready to let the universe help you be your own Saving Grace? Let's go!

Here are 15 steps to the happiness, joy and peace you are entitled to … Read them and see what resonates with you. Then as the great writer, Deborah Levy, once told me on a beautiful island in Greece … "Start where you like".

Part 1: LEARN TO LOVE YOURSELF

Step 1: Get motivated! … let the universe get you going.

Nothing happens by accident. Coincidence doesn't exist. Serendipity – things happening by chance for our benefit - rules. That doesn't mean it makes sense at the time … or feels fair, or even good. But sometimes the universe, in an act of unexpected and un-noticed kindness, puts you in a place where you knock a pebble off the top of a gentle, unassuming slope in the sun … and before you know it you are living an avalanche. Not one that will suffocate you, even more than you are already choking from life's apparent unjustness. No. One that will wipe clear anything in your way that is making you live from a place of fear, not love; moving aside obstacles to your happiness, and relentlessly making a path for deserved, selfless happiness … and peace. One pebble.

Unknowingly, I found the pebble that would lead to me learning to love myself in August 2014. I wasn't beach-combing. Well not consciously. I didn't do anything consciously at all that summer. 2014 would bring the summer my kids saw their mum cry. And cry. And cry. Well into the Autumn. I still remember the day I emailed a good friend of mine that Autumn, to say I was celebrating 30 days without crying... it was sometime later in November. Sadly, she too was familiar with depression and had previously helped me identify that I also was. You need friends like that, as when people are in a dark place, it is harder for them to shed light on their situation alone.

So, in August I was shelf-combing. Calm but numb. Wandering stupefied through the lovely Algarve house, lent to me by a friend for low-cost holidays befitting my unemployed teacher's non-existent salary. The house was quiet, as the children slept after yet another glorious late night in the flood-lit pool in the cricket-bombastic gardens, filled with trees bearing local delights: almonds, figs and oranges. We had had an even more glorious afternoon at Ancao Beach, watching the sun set, the Algarve sand cooling under our toes, while my chest warmed with South American sugar cane Caipirinha, served by the friendly bar-owner of the "Dois Mocos" beach bar.

That morning the terracotta tiles under my de-hydrated, neglected, dry-skinned soles, weren't rough enough to wake me from my half-stupor. But I was lucid enough to scan, even criticise, the contents of the 1970's bamboo bookshelf. Seriously, who still did bamboo? (There it goes – judgement.) Then my eyes, just recovering from the previous night's post-beach dinner, sipping Portugal's finest Planalto, paused. Despite a double honours degree from a Russell group University in French and German, I have never been a great reader. But I love scouring a bookshelf, in the vain hope that in a next life, perhaps retirement, I will sit by the sea and read endlessly, my grey, curly hair blowing in the wind, while the sand tickles my toes ...

My eyes found a black and white spine. "How do you want me?", it read ... Oh, the plethora of connotations that raced through my 9am pre-coffee mind, from naughty teenager in that very region 30 years earlier ... to more recent, racy nights, as a 40 something singleton. My fingers were pulled, slightly bored and without resistance, to the 1cm wide, vertical paper saviour. Ruby had found me.

Hours and pages later, countries and worlds apart, it all came back to Roehampton, where I had grown up. And the Priory, where so many have sought peace. Ruby Wax, in her transparent, self-aware, self-revealing loveliness, made it known to herself, and to the world, that it's OK and actually quite wise, to know that you aren't OK. But she is so damn clever (not to mention funny), that she didn't need anyone else to tell her so. Go RUBY. She chose the next step alone. Despite her OCD mum, her Frankfurter-mobile-driving dad and her own buck teeth, she admitted to us all, I'm not OK, and that's OK. Thank you Ruby. That day I too realised it was OK not be OK. And I made a promise to myself to change things there and then. The last four years my life had been on pause and it was time to press play ...

Let me explain and back track to 2010 (See question 13 above). For years I had convinced myself that I was ok ... and better off alone. That it was my choice to be alone. I had after all been the one to expel my husband from the house, on hearing that, out of the blue, he wouldn't be joining me and his family in London. 'I am not walking away from my project' he'd affirmed, when confronted by his incredulous wife in our taupe and cappuccino kitchen. Project, I had thought, project! Building a 5-star resort in a country in ruins for a soon-to-be-bankrupt, fraudulent company, that had caused our financial, and consequently marital demise. Project! "What about THIS project" I had protested, gesturing around me at our beautiful home and even more beautiful children, aged just 3, 6 and 9. Big-eyed. Beautiful. "THIS is MY project... OUR project."

Silence. As usual, silence. My still, dumb-founded, unbelieving, non-believing body, was soundless on the designer, rubber floor we had picked together seven years earlier, when we were blissfully happy parents of one 18-month-old girl. Now his 6-foot, 80 kg frame that left the house and with it our 18-year journey, was totally imperceptible. Despite the weight of the act on my life, it made not a single ripple in the fabric of the Earlsfield universe. Not. A. Ripple. The 1930's Edwardian door lock clicked almost inaudibly as my gentle sobs began to be heard.

And so it began; my determined journey to prove to my future ex-husband and the world that I wasn't an unnoticed ripple. I was a fucking unstoppable tsunami. I didn't need him, or want anyone for that matter. My despondent heart had, unawares, allowed his gesture of avoidance, apathy and apparent weakness, to spark embers of pain in me ... to fuel anxiety-driven rage ... hell hath no fury ... LIKE A MINDLESS, BROKEN, FEMALE HEART ...

As my 'rock' moved silently away from me, like many hurt souls before me, I began my tearful obsession with the question: why?

29

Why me? Why us? Why my family? More than anything in the world, I had wished to have and raise a big, happy family, full of the hustle and bustle, life and laughter, I had so craved for myself as a child, often alone in a quiet, council flat, with my family a thousand miles away. And for a decade it looked like I had achieved my dream, despite the bumps on the way. But now that dream lay in tatters with me on the kitchen floor.

It's actually quite hard to tap into what went on in the hurt years that followed. When your amygdala (your survival instinct) is steering you, your hippocampus (the bit that helps you remember past mistakes) can't. At least this is the science I tell my students nowadays. So the next two years of hurt, spent on 'tigress alert', focussed solely on keeping our, no my, babies, from harm. For two years until he actually came back to the UK and was physically, though not mentally, on the same island, my sole purpose from waking until sleeping, was to make sure they were fed, smiling, warm … and oblivious. Oblivious to the fact that history had repeated itself. That their mother who had herself been raised by a single mother, was alone and raising them as a single mum 35 years later.

A numb, monotonous routine soon set in. Every two weeks he would fly over to spend the weekend at the house, banished from our bed to one of the children's. My icy façade would have frozen anything that dared touch me. Luckily my sharp tongue kept everyone at bay. Occasionally it thawed, as the warmth of finding the five of us in a room together laughing, reminded me that there was still love there. But as the time approached at the end of each visit for him to leave once more, my steeliness would return. My self-defence system would re-emerge and nothing could melt it until his plane had taken off and put miles between us again. Miles that had existed between us for years in our conversations, now existed in our bodies. As if the physical plane was finally catching up with the unspoken spiritual one.

And so time passed for those first six months of our separation. Despite the drain on my emotions, by body was able to continue. Bodies do that. They stay standing, on automatic pilot, allowing you to survive and press on as you have to, even though your heart and soul just want to stop everything. It must be what keeps soldiers going, even when they are exhausted and war-torn.

My heartache was buried deep under outward waves of energy. For her 9th birthday I traipsed up to North London, literally to the end of the line, to get my eldest daughter two kittens. Because that's what you need when you are tidying and cleaning alone after three kids; two extra mouths to feed and bottoms to clean! And to make sure he wouldn't miss out on what the other boys had with their dads each weekend, I enrolled my six-year-old son in not one but two sports each weekend. I still shudder when I recall his tiny legs, used to the warm Lisbon climate, bare and goose-bumped in little black shorts, as he raced around the football and rugby pitches of middle-class Wandsworth Common, while I stood as proud as any of the dads (and many other mums too) by the side-lines. My feet almost as frozen as my heart.

As for my youngest, to this day she says she has no memory of living with her father at all. It was like salt on the wound. Having learnt Portuguese as her first language, she soon forgot every word and every memory of the two houses she had lived in there.

SW18 was her new home, alone with mum, and of all of them, she settled in the easiest. Having been raised playing on the sandy shores in Cascais, she soon became accustomed to playing in the sand pits of the Wandsworth nursery playground.

I am still amazed by the trust that those three young souls showed in me and in the world, as they found themselves in a new place and with a new family dynamic. No-one moaned. No-one questioned. I must have been doing something right, even if I felt inside that I was clutching at straws. Often, we judge and berate ourselves for being bad parents, when, given what we are coping with, we are actually doing a bloody good job. But the human brain is built to criticise. Luckily it also has defence mechanisms, which kept my kids going happily (for now).

By that first 'single' Spring back in the UK in 2011, I was desperate to become financially independent. Fed up with working in the world of interiors, where builders make a promise to complete something, when all they make is a cup of tea, within six months I reached back out for the first time in eight years to the world of HR. Without wanting to appear smug, I am proud to say that I have been offered every job I have been interviewed for. Getting every job you go for, however, especially when you've only been looking for a few days, without really thinking things through, can be anything but a blessing. Before I knew it, I had signed on the dotted line to work four days a week in a prestigious department store I had never even been inside before the day of the interview. I hadn't really thought things through AT ALL. After eight years running my own interior design business, I felt the need to be able to increase my independence, to be able to raise a mortgage alone, sensing my impending divorce. So, I returned to the wonderful world of Human Resources (or Human Remains as it is affectionately called). The industry, the culture, the hours, were all new to me, but in true me-style, I had had an urge and followed it, impulsively and with great haste and modesty-aside, success. Years later as I write this, I shudder at the old me and count my blessings for what I have learnt since then. But without regrets.

Every part of our journey has a role to play. Even those hideous ten months brought me some learning; how to evaluate what is important to you and work towards TRUE, FELT JOY & HAPPINESS. One day, shortly after joining THE STORE known for its bright yellow bags, I was leading my team's 'getting to know you' workshop. When asked what success meant to her, one of my lovely team members said, simply ... to be happy. As others in the room shared dreams of leading departments in some of the world's best department stores, she was happy to 'settle' for mere happiness. There was something incredibly humble and warming there, that I now see as so much more than 'settling'. Thank you Helen, you are a wise soul. At the time my judgement was too clouded to see it, but the message was received, eventually.

Another of the many things I have come to understand, is that under pressure or out of fear, we all do what we can, with the skills and courage we have at that time. There is no point in regretting things you have done. You can't undo them. You can only use them to guide you in your next steps. Everything in life is a lesson. And there is no point in hating others for things they have done, as they too could only use the tools and tenacity they had at the point of action. You might never forget when someone has hurt you, but it's much easier, and healthier, to forgive them for acting out of fear not love, than holding onto hatred and spite. And once you get strong again, as I did after finding Ruby's pivotal publication, you might even be able to share the light of your love with others, so that they might be able to change; so that they might let go of THEIR fear and start acting from the love too.

It is worth mentioning however, that the universe didn't exactly make things easy for me during those ten months at the Materialistic Mecca. Seven months into the separation and just two weeks into the new job, I had the fortune to be invited to a friend's 40th in Spain. I flew there from London and settled into my room. Enjoyed the pre-party celebrations. My future-ex drove all 800km from Lisbon (always keen to save money, as his work would pay his petrol but not his flight). The main event was, as expected, amazing. A fabulous gathering of old friends, girls all attired in gorgeous cocktail gowns and gents in black-tie (who can resist a man in a tux?). We sipped Champagne and Aperol around the pool with its Moroccan décor, dined, then more bubbles. As was expected, many of us ended up in the pool well into the early hours of the morning (if I recall correctly, a few pairs of shoes and even an iPhone went for a dip too). Not as expected, however, once I had walked the 50m back to my hotel, no sooner had I settled into my bed, than a knock at the door was heard. A cheeky smile I recognised only too well greeted me when I opened. After a merry evening of fun, laughter and celebration among friends, made all the merrier by bottles of bubbles, the fervently independent and determined me vanished, for a night of love, that made the previous months seem as if they had never happened. I can hear your murmurs of distraught disapproval as

I write, but seven months is a long time to feel lonely.

Another thing that I have learnt, is that after a 'high' there often comes a low. In this case a crash. A plummeting into an abyss. I have read that one explanation could be that we are so incredulous of our good fortune, of the positive turn of events, that our doubt and fear is actually strong enough to bring about the end of this high. Our anticipation that good times won't last or that we don't deserve them, can actually bring an end to the loving and joyous sensations at the peak.

Whatever you believe, for just 48 hours, I was back in love and truly believed our separation had ended, when he said at Malaga airport that he would indeed come back to the UK (after closing a few things back in Lisbon). My grin didn't drop for two days, as I let every muscle in my body relax for the first time in ages and wallow in the thought that love had conquered. We would be a family once again. I was able to walk back to work with a spring in my step, light with love. But that lightness was soon replaced with lead, as the promises turned to empty lies on his next fortnightly visit to the UK. It still baffles me how, after knowing someone for over twenty years, I could misjudge them so monumentally. How could I have been such a sucker to think that the night of Spanish sex was actually heart felt, and not just a drunken romp after months of abstinence? And if I was hurt and defensive after the first revelation back in October 2010, after this second blow, my walls were even higher and stronger. But the soul that hid behind them was even more broken. By the time Ruby's book would find me three years later, the shattered pieces would be countless.

Back to London in 2011 and to THE STORE; a place where plenty of people worked from a place of fear. Fear to lag behind fashion trends. Fear to be fired by ruthless bosses. Fear that life without a thousand-pound handbag would appear less worthy. Unfortunately, it turned out not to be the best move for me. My wardrobe acquired more little black dresses, and designer handbags (NOT at a thousand pounds, I hasten to add) and even a pair of patent black heels (which have since been donated). And my friends were able to take full advantage of amazing discounts, although how paying £300 for a blender is a bargain, I don't know. As Madonna sang, we live in a material world. And although my bank balance rose, my heart sank further.

Luckily, despite being new to the job, I had insisted that my contract include two weeks off in August to join the children, who were on holiday with their father in Portugal. On arrival I was instantly shocked to hear that a very close friend of mine had divorced her husband. Still believing I would find a way to save my own marriage, I saw her situation as much worse than mine – ironic, given that she has been happy ever since her drastic and speedy decision, whereas I would take another three years to achieve the same. And having spent the last year separated without a thought of divorce paperwork, I found it hard to take in how she had managed to leave and divorce her husband in just ninety days. Being a lawyer herself had no doubt helped. That and the heart-break driven determination that I saw in her eyes, when we (all 5 of us) drove to Santa Cruz beach to meet her. Although people do not necessarily go through all of them or experience them in the same order, there are five stages of grief; Denial and Isolation; Anger; Bargaining; Depression; and

Acceptance. And all bar the last are stages where we live in a place of fear, not love. My fearless friend had managed to avoid the first four and go straight to number five, enabling herself to heal in a way I have never seen. And she has not faltered until this day. Amazing.

Anyway, that Summer holiday back in 2011, I was back at stage one and by the end of the first week, had been joined by an apparently amenable 'husband' and we were holidaying like the perfect family. It was Spain all over again. And more. My guard was down. Packed up and bundled away into the loft, I would even dare to say. There was no hiding of anything. If they weren't so young, I would call them as witnesses that he gave an Oscar-winning performance as the prodigal father. It was as if the last twelve months hadn't happened. We spent seven glorious days playing happy families. I wasn't quite as joyous as I had been in Spain – perhaps I knew something deep down – but I was happy. There was no bitterness in my words, no spite. I think having seen my friend's marriage end, had softened me and made me more willing to compromise. The thing is, what you often end up compromising is your self-esteem. For, sure as you will be telling yourselves as you read this, after a week back under our marital sheets and back in our family's life, low and behold he revealed that actually he wasn't quite ready to leave 'the project'. The kids and I were second class yet again. And I felt bottom of the pile. Perhaps you know that feeling?

In hindsight I wonder whether his ego kicked in. It does that. Starts telling you not to take risks, when you try and make changes. Even if they are positive ones. Maybe his ego said 'lovely holiday, but don't be fooled. The nagging will soon be back'. Who knows. Irrelevant now.

I don't know how I managed to come back from that one. As I said earlier, when you have no other choice, you plod on. And God knows what the kids thought of it all. I was too numb to notice or ask and to tell the truth, I can't remember. Like me, they came back to London and slipped back into the life they knew. The initial confidence that had enabled me to shine my way into the job five months earlier, shaken first by the grand Granada deception and now, torn apart by the Algarve earthquake, wore off completely. Unlike the lipstick of the immaculately groomed people working around me. Having previously been commended for 'getting things done', by Christmas I found myself struggling to complete tasks well below my professional ability. I was sinking into incompetence and into a depression. Sadness is like that. What starts off as feeling a bit of low here and there, unremedied, can funnel down and become exhaustion and depressions. More about that in the second part of the book.

As if my broken heart wasn't enough, I was forced to watch my children's break too. The birthday cats had mated at Easter and produced three beautiful kittens before the summer. For a few months the house was filled with the joy that comes with new, fluffy life. But like I said, after some highs ... you crash. No sooner had the children returned from a long summer in the sun, desperate to be reunited with their fluff-balls, than the mother cat came down with a sudden virus that crippled her. At first, we thought it was just exhaustion from feeding her hungry litter while she herself was only a year old. But when her back legs failed her, a trip to the vet soon revealed an irreversible condition. Without pet insurance, I was forced to throw much-needed money at the situation, in the vain attempt to save her life and my children from heartache. I struggled to juggle phone calls to the vet, with pressures at work, as I was being pressed to decide whether to burn even more money in what was apparently incurable. But how could I agree to the alternative – to ending the life of the cat, who for a year had crept under my daughter's duvet and curled up next to her like a living, breathing teddy bear? It felt like an eternity, but the fatal deterioration and final extermination took place in just 48 hours. No one had the time to absorb what was going on, least of all my winded babes, who were just four, seven and ten. Keen to give them the opportunity to say farewell to Juliet, I took them all to the vet that last evening. Their eyebrows raised in horror to see her paralysed from the waist down, moving in circles, as she attempted to get closer to them. But brave as soldiers, they stroked her and consoled her with soothing words. In my mind I had made it clear that she wouldn't make it and that it was the only and kind thing we could do to have her put down. But as I came back into the reception area having witnessed her life being extinguished, and told them she was gone, the disbelief in their eyes made it obvious that I hadn't been clear enough.

Nowadays, when teaching Mindfulness to children, I say that, like weebles, people wobble but we don't fall down. But that day fall down they did. It is hard to describe the pain I felt as I watched the older two cry non-stop for two hours on the sofa at home, as their younger sister watched on, too young to grasp what had happened. But as mean as the universe might seem, the experience was not without lightness. Human beings crave fitting in with the norm. While her siblings sobbed, my youngest got out her colouring pencils and after a while I was presented with a picture of a child crying. "Mummy," she beckoned, inappropriately cheerfully for the occasion, but wonderfully guilt-free, as any four-year-old should be. Proudly holding out her work of art, she added "This is what I would look like if I was sad."

Mindfulness teaches us that difficult feelings come when we allow ourselves to interpret events negatively and react emotionally, rather than respond objectively and with equanimity. These interpretations are learnt, born of value systems that people hand down to us. In my experience, having taught over 4500 of them, children are naturally mindful until they become fearful. That day my daughter showed me that it was possible to remain unshaken, despite the situation. While her two siblings, having experienced uncertainty and loss, were controlled by their ruminating thoughts that they would never see the cat again, Lara stayed present. Her youth offered her the ability to remain unscathed by the attachment her brother and sister were suffering from, and to refrain from projecting herself into a cat-less future, as they were so whole-heartedly doing. While they were distraught in their thinking, she was just being.

Of course, it is easy for me to say that now, many years after discovering Ruby's autobiography and the path it guided me towards. Back in 2011 I too was not being. I was just doing, day in and day out, from the day I asked him to leave in October 2010, until the day I found out he had a new love in June 2014. Three and a half years of thinking, analysing, rationalising, ruminating. Hankering over a past that I was so attached to, it took a crow bar to yank me away from it. But first I had to be yanked away from the very life that was preventing me from being.

Yet another of the many lessons I have learnt, is that every person you meet is sent to you for a reason. That Autumn, as Christmas 2011 approached I became more and more incapable at work and more and more down in life, to the point where after work I would cry myself from the station to my front door in sheer relief that another day was nearly over. Still able to put on some measure of appearances, I managed to keep to most routines. It's funny. When you go to your GP and tell them you are sad, they ask you to fill in a questionnaire to ascertain how much your sadness is just that, or whether you are actually 'depressed'. One key question is (roughly) to what extent does your mood interfere with your daily life and your ability to carry out daily tasks. Now, when you are a single mother of three, you have little choice but to get up, get them to school, get yourself to work, get back, feed, bathe and settle them in bed each day. So, my answer was always, it doesn't interfere. Therefore, I was not depressed. But the week before Christmas the sensation of suffocating in my chest was growing. Each day I dreaded going in to work the next day. One might be mistaken to believe that I was just unhappy with my job, or scared of my boss. But it was more than that. I was living in a perpetual state of unease and was unable to see a way out.

That is when the universe sent me a life-jacket in the shape of a fellow parent from my son's class. Drowning as I was in anxiety, I carried on as if nothing was wrong by meeting with girlfriends for a drink at the local pub for some 'me-time' while mum babysat. Some might scoff at the excuse of 'me-time' that mums often 'whinge' about, but it is scientifically proven to be critical for our wellbeing (men and women). Back in the days when we had to fight sabre-tooth tigers, a life-style that would have us living on almost permanent amygdala-fuelled adrenalin, we would release all the harmful chemicals as we gathered by the evening open fire and chanted or played drums (you get the picture). Nowadays, there are no sabre-tooth tigers at our door, although a trek around the supermarket to hunt and gather can be hideously stressful. Nevertheless, our lives are filled with stress. Will we get the kids to school on time? Are the kids happy at school? Are we finding the best bargains to save money? Will our jobs be there tomorrow? Will we be able to pay the mortgage? Are we keeping up with the Joneses? …. The list of real or self-imposed pressures builds up in us, filling us with vicious chemicals, that, if not expelled from our bodies, will drive us to an early grave. So, gather at the pub we must. To share our worries over Sauvignon Blanc and safeguard our sanity.

So, one evening, mid-season-of-goodwill, I openly and frankly shared my unhappiness about my work, when my wise friend Emily, to whom I am forever grateful, said simply "Call the doctor and get her to sign you off work". The thought of not standing up to a challenge or letting go of my responsibilities was totally alien to me, but I was so desperate to catch my breath that the next morning, at 8am, I did just that. I had been to see the GP earlier that term, so I guess she felt the despair in my voice, as she didn't hesitate to send the required letter. Then I emailed my bosses to say that I wouldn't be in for three weeks. Three whole weeks. It was all so simple. So simple. And then I breathed …

Unlike wise Ruby, however, I hadn't realised how low I had sunk. As I let go of my duty to turn up at work, I let go of all the stress and strain and the weight lifted from my chest. I banished any thoughts of guilt from my mind and in hindsight I must have been showing my low mood at work much more than I was aware, as my colleagues were surprisingly not taken aback by my overnight disappearance. Sometimes a belief that the world can't go on without us, that we are indispensable, is what stops us from doing what our minds need most. The world of retail didn't implode in my absence and rather than be hurt by my apparent lack of importance, I took it as a green light to focus on what I wanted and my family needed.

'Fortune favours the bold' is another of the many lessons I have learnt. It took some courage for me not to go to work but during those three weeks, I reconnected with my children. I indulged us all in present-moment, family time – I got my breath back and they got their mum back (for a short while at least). And I was rewarded with the life-changing realisation that being around children, and more specifically, teaching them, was what I really wanted to do. I would become a teacher.

As I said earlier, serendipity rules. That Christmas my eldest happened to be preparing for two dreaded 10+ exams. The pressure was slightly on, as I was quite clear with her, yet gently so, that we would only be able to afford a private school if she got a scholarship. What will be, will be, I told her. Looking back now as a Mindfulness-based 11+ tutor, I shake my head at my former self and the stress that must have been for her. But I am also compassionate enough with myself now to know that I shared that with her, in order to soften any blow that might come. I was determined to prepare her for the worst: getting in but not affording it. Talk about wishing for something and in the same breath not believing in it, so potentially wishing it away! Luckily my cautious self was accompanied by my bold self, even then. Against all odds and her doubting father, I filled in reams of bursary application forms and set to teaching her the art of essay-writing.

Given how hard it was sometimes to spend nine minutes with her in her middle years, frosty teen that she could be (although the arrival of a lovely boyfriend enabled a glacial thaw), my cheeks rise and my heart warms as I recall the nine hours we spent together over those three days in January 2012. My then clearer head was able to, untrained, intuitively, break down the art of creating an interesting beginning, a climaxing middle and a conclusive ending. Little did I know that I was myself completing my own interesting beginning and soon to embark on a climaxing middle, of MY story. All it took was 540 minutes of vitalising verbs, active adverbs and awesome adjectives to discover my passion for helping a child turn a blank page into a gripping, descriptive story, that makes them blush with pride. Before my three week 'sabbatical' was over, I had sent a letter of resignation, investigated where to do my teacher training and signed up for work experience at the children's school. Mummy was back off to Uni in the Autumn!

As Jon Kabat-Zinn says wisely, it's the 'awareness that arises from paying attention on purpose in the present moment, non-judgmentally'. In those nine hours tutoring Nina, I paid attention to our experience, with the sole purpose of helping her flourish, judging neither my teaching nor her writing skills. And the result was enlightening awareness; I wanted to teach children. That's the power of Mindfulness.

Thanks to Emily's wise words at the watering hole and my new-found breath, the winds of change cleared the cobwebs of my low mood.

The Universe was beginning to motivate me, to get me going.

For six months I amused myself at the thought of becoming a teacher. Apparently there are three types of teacher. First, those who have known since early childhood that they wanted to teach and spent hours lining up their teddies in 'classrooms' on the carpet of their bedrooms, teaching them to count and putting them in the corner if they misbehaved. Then there are those who enjoy their subject so much at University that they decide to pass their love on to the generations that follow. Then there are people like me. Who, often around the age of a 'midlife-crisis', disillusioned by an unfulfilling career or driven be a desire to give something back to society, abandon their payslip and walk through the student union bar doors once more. Only this time it wasn't a pound a pint!

Actually, when I reflected on it, as you do when you have to pinch yourself to realise you aren't dreaming that you are back in a lecture room, I realised that I had come full circle in a way. Out of fear of not earning enough or not keeping up with my friends, 15 years earlier I had left a job I loved, where my role was to teach others to be the best they could (as hotel supervisors and managers, then consultants then bankers). Then in September 2012, I found myself once again facilitating learning, motivating strugglers, fast-tracking the able. Teaching once again. And loving it once again. I chose to teach from a place of love, not fear. Those choices are the ones that work. And although the greatest turbulence was yet to come, this calm before the storm gave me a chance to reconnect with a passion and build some resilience for the dark days ahead.

Ruby was able to hide behind her comedy until she could hide no longer. Similarly, I hid behind my albeit interesting PGCE from 2012-2013 and the first exhilarating term as a teacher in late 2013, until I too could hide no longer. The first part was easy. With him finally back in the UK from August 2012 and living at my mother's at the end of the road, life became much easier. We tried for over a year to make things work. Trying looked like dinner at the house then a Swedish drama on TV. Nothing more. Each of us waiting for something to click. Funny how after two decades together, something as simple as sitting on the sofa can be awkward. By now he too was low. Two years of living out of a suitcase at my uncle's house in Lisbon before returning to his mother-in-laws and to a grey, monotonous commute, compared to the sunny sand dunes of 'the project', would have been enough to make anyone depressed. Recognising this, and coming from a place of love, I foolishly suggested he rent a flat. I knew even then that no one can be in a good place to rekindle love, if they aren't happy themselves. So, I selflessly encouraged him to get a place, truly wishing him to be strong and happy, so that we might find our happiness together again. How naïve. Heart-felt but naïve.

Having found a flat nearby, he found his self-esteem soon enough. For a short while, three months maybe, we were getting on better than ever, despite my stress as an NQT teacher. I would even dare to say we got close to getting back together. While his confidence was being boosted by his personal space in his pretty pad, mine was being destroyed by my new boss. I was being scrutinised, criticised, bullied, effectively. I was miserable and even shared this with a teacher at my children's school but was encouraged not to give up. And true to my name, I heeded that advice. Where there's a Wille, there's a way. However, by Christmas Eve the level of anxiety building up in me was near boiling point, as I worked eleven hours at the school then another three or four hours at home after the kids were asleep, marking and planning lessons. I knew the children and parents at my school loved me, but the Head was set against me. And then the moment came when the kettle would blow its whistle, the pot would blow its lid and I would blow my marriage. All the pain I had experienced from the age of two – some of it still unknown and some just ignored or buried – what rise to the surface and explode in a torrent of destruction. Pain does that; if you don't deal with it, like a dormant volcano, it does nothing for ages, until one day it can erupt.

And all because of frozen profiteroles. I still laugh when I think about it. In fact, I still laugh every time I buy them (the nice, fresh ones, of course). He had been given one job, that Xmas, just ONE. Bring dessert. I was doing the main. A friend was bringing starters and he had been allocated dessert. I had seen a beautiful selection at Marks and Spencer earlier that day (divine star-shaped chocolate mousses and tall towers of profiteroles, bathed in rich chocolate sauce with golden sprinkles), but as it wasn't my part of the meal and I was trying to learn to let go and be less of a control-freak, I hadn't bought them. Exhausted after the Ofsted inspection and the longest term of the school year, I dragged myself towards Christmas just about in one piece. At least on the surface. Then I saw them. The Sainsbury's 'basics' frozen profiteroles that were to be our Christmas dessert. The orange and white box of 'economy' grade dessert, hard and chocolate-free. There is no excuse for what I did next, and I am to this day regretful and sorry. A torrent of abuse burst from my mouth. An unstoppable wave of insults and accusations of mediocrity flowed and flowed and flowed. I felt as if I was watching myself from the other side of the kitchen, powerless. Unable to stop this hurt, broken woman from verbally destroying the man she loved and thus causing her own self-destruction.

He left. Of course he did. Rightly so in one way. He reacted out of hurt and fear. Fear to have to take more abuse. But what if he had read Ruby's book first. What if he had breathed in the face of my abuse. What if, strong in the knowledge that every word I said I was actually saying about myself, he had been able to act out of love. All I needed was a hug. All I needed was to hear that it would be ok. That my job would be okay. That WE would be ok. But everything happens for a reason and people can only use the tools they have. He didn't have those tools. And I needed to realise I, not just our marriage, was broken and needed to fix myself. The door clicked as he shut it, just as it had two years earlier. And I knew then that there was no turning back.

Sure, I (or at least my brain in subconscious denial mode) tried to ignore that knowledge for another six months as he moved further away from me. I carried on inviting him over for dinner with the children, but the rejections became more frequent. I sensed there might be someone new in his life. Even joked about it in front of the kids (doh!). But this time it was me who was giving an Oscar-winning performance at school and at home, pretending I was ok. I even had a few dates in a half-hearted attempt to show the world I was moving on. But when the final, unavoidable blow came and he revealed he was seeing someone, there was nowhere to hide. I made a desperate last attempt to persuade him we were meant to be; I made an album of our 22 years together and gave it to him on what would have been our 14th wedding anniversary. Fear of the end and attachment to a love I at least still felt, refused to do the sensible thing and step down so I could take stock; instead it gave me boundless adrenalin to keep trying. But it was too little, too late. For us at least. For me it was just the beginning.

That summer I set off to Portugal as usual with the last scraps of energy and bravado I could muster. I had to go on. And what better than the sun and the sea to make you forget. To help you take the first steps on a long, windy road of healing. Someone or something up there must have been listening and feeling generous. Really generous, because by the time I came back I felt a little revived. Sure the tan and the beach-toned body showed the world a revitalised me, but more importantly I felt a new resilient me growing inside – sometimes painfully slowly, and with plenty of steps backwards – but there. The mere first feather of the phoenix to come.

So back to finding that autobiography on the shelf. Resilience must be Ruby's middle name. In my eyes at least. In the book she is brutally and hilariously honest about her unhappy childhood, where she appears constantly put down by her OCD mother and embarrassed by her father, with the odd frankfurter-shaped van he would pick her up from school in. As I reread it out loud to my children as they lay by the pool that summer in 2014, it reminded me of how I would shudder with embarrassment at 3.30pm in the 80's and pretend my mother, their grandmother, had forgotten to pick me up, having spotted her from behind the school gates with mad silver stripes down her jet black hair, from an event the night before at the restaurant she worked in. Ruby's trials with her buck teeth also reminded me of how, as a teenager with not just 'railway track' braces but also a head brace, my brother would tease me and say I looked like an American football player in bed each night.

But as mentioned earlier, I wasn't consciously unhappy as a child. While the seeds of some insecurities were definitely planted during my childhood, my personal breakdown was caused by the loss of a man I loved more than he will ever know (unless he reads the copy he's been given). But thanks to Ruby and her serendipitous appearance on the bookshelf, my recovery, my self-rediscovery, was also enabled by this thing we call Mindfulness. As I saw myself in her and saw how she led herself to her recovery, I was encouraged to do the same, as I hope this book will encourage you. Her humour brought me laughter I hadn't heard in years. The similarities between us reminded me no one is alone in the world. As I read her book under the bright August sun, it was all the light I needed to turn my back on sadness. The Universe had done its magic and I was motivated to get happy. Here's what I did next ...

Step 2: Get clean! : wash away any low vibrations

"You're so lucky!" is what you hear from married girlfriends, when you tell them you have a week kid-free by the beach. Really? Not so much lucky as ... desperately seeking significant ways to fill your time, when the three things that make up the essence of your being have been time-shared with a once-best-friend-husband-now-future-ex ...

After a dozen years of holidays that involved making baby-mush that won't dry up or go off in the heat, of trying to rock your child to sleep for her afternoon nap under the parasol, while judgmental brown eyes (above bulging black swimwear) glare at you, oozing how bad a parent you are for having your child out in the midday heat (don't they know how little sunlight we get in the UK?) ... only to get an hour's rest (if you're lucky) to read the stupid book you bought at the airport, (why, oh why, did you buy a self-help book? Bring on the Joanna Trollope or Jackie Collins) .... (breathe) ... after all THAT, a week in the sun kid-free can be ... well ... uncrowded.

But then that's where friends come in. Some people come into your life for no apparent reason, yet as I've said already, now I know it is never for no reason. As my friend's four-wheel drive pulled up at Lisbon airport on that August evening, over two hours' drive from her amazing (think Grand Designs) home to the South, I sighed. For once Jose Mourinho's face on a poster wasn't staring at me at the pick-up point at arrivals, 4m tall, as he had been for the last half dozen years. Billboards could really do better to promote Portugal's finest specimens. Maybe Ronaldo in his underwear range ...

Anyway it wasn't a HEAVY sigh. Just a sigh. An 'I'm at my other home' kind of sigh, which will resonate with anyone with foreign parents or dual nationality, who has their heart split across borders. Arriving at Lisbon airport has always been, and continues to be, a mood-defining moment. One that you can't pre-empt until you are there. More precise than therapy (of which I have had none yet), it pinpoints exactly where I am at that point in my life, purely by how I react to coming out of the automatic sliding doors – only then can I tell 'who' has arrived.

It's an event that captures my state of mind year after year ... no, decade after decade. If I let my memory wander back to the late seventies, I see me and my brother wearing our huge 'unaccompanied minors' white plastic pouches around our necks, with large green and red letters on them saying 'TAP U.M.' We had each other, so we weren't really unaccompanied. Not since the day he was born five weeks early in December in 1971, with the whole family at Bethlehem, sorry I mean Barnet, to witness the coming of the messy-iah (and messy he has been, at times). Had anyone from Portugal or Germany bothered to pitch up for my more timely arrival on the cusp of Virgo and Libra? Of course not! Only the hospital-cleaner, who had found mum almost delivering her first born in the loo, was aware of the urgency of my arrival.

Still thinking about the past, Ed and I have always accompanied each other. Willingly or not. He was there on the shop door step, when I stole his doughnut aged two, singing sweetly "poor baby".

In revenge, he was there years later, when a worm (at the end of a stick he was holding) was getting up close and personal with my nose hairs in SW19, while not a single adult noticed me being harassed by a worm-holding worm of a little brother. And he was there when, at the grand old age of twelve, with not a grand-parent or mother in sight, I started my path to woman-hood. We were playing chess in the caravan, after a hard day cart-wheeling and wave-jumping at the beach in Cacela. Me 12. Him 10. We were just chilling, no stress. "Anna, I think your bikini's bleeding" he'd remarked. Me, "Oh, so it is... Check mate!"

Where was I? Oh yes ... Lisbon airport, 2014, 7pm, one August evening, roughly 2 months after I had found out that my separated husband of 21 years (aka best friend, and father of my 3 beautiful kids, who deserved better), had been seeing someone else for anything up to 6 months, because frankly, "we didn't make each other happy", he'd claimed. Sadly, he still hadn't seen that 'we' as a couple weren't the issue; our individual depressions (mine visible, his hidden well behind his ever-neutral façade) were masquerading as a broken marriage and gave an Oscar-winning performance, which led to the end of the world as we knew it. Hindsight is great. At least it's better than never waking up to the truth. But that is someone else's journey. Someone else's path to tread. Not my bag to carry.

So my great friend pulls up. Car brimming with Zara Home bags for her new, now well-known and fabulous 'harmony escape' luxury eco-resort. Halfway across the stunning, never-ending, cable-stayed bridge across the River Tagus (spot the ex-wife of a civil engineer), I started to cry. No crisis. After all, it's all I'd been doing for the last two months. Sixty days of crying since the day

I, having just found out I had a potentially life-threatening virus, worrying I would die of cancer and leave my three beautiful babes, had turned up at the local shopping centre, and asked him for a reconciliation for the seventh time in three years. Sixty days of crying since I had heard he was seeing someone and, with his new hoover in hand and habitual lop-sided, dimpled, gorgeous, grin on face, heard him say "I'm happy". Sixty days of tears since that day. So, as we drove over the muddy waters of the Tagus, I cried my salty tears. I didn't sob. They just trickled ... mourned their way down my suntanned cheeks. As the landscape turned from suburb to savannah, my very slow, tired, tears dried, retreated. "We're here", she whispered. "Paraiso Escondido" (Hidden Paradise). You'll be ok. Just breathe."

The purpose of the trip was to feed my soul, to start loving myself again. A month alone with the children had allowed for too much introspection time, despite levity brought by Ruby's revelations. Too much thinking and not enough being. Too much ruminating about what I had done wrong and how I could get him back, and not enough sensing. It was time to clear the mist and find the path ahead. And up on that beautiful Alentejo hill you could see for miles around. As you stood amid the eucalyptus trees, and filled your chest with the scented air, pushing every rib as far as you could, your shoulders dropped with every exhalation and your worries dropped with them. There you could see the wood for the trees.

Uncharacteristically I hadn't planned anything for those five days – in my increasingly obvious depression, my uber-organised-self had given way to a more drift-like way of being. Originally I was going to help her unpack into her new home.

However, as the cement floor still wasn't dry, she was free to devote her time to me and my wet tears instead. I had no idea what was about to unfold. Despite her Catholic upbringing and faith, she had developed a strong sense of spirituality and belief in the Universe and its ways. The Portuguese are predominantly a Catholic people, but the Alentejo is also steeped in its own beliefs and superstition; the thick walls of the tiny white houses, with typical azure-blue borders, keep out the heat and keep in old traditions, that few outsiders ever hear of. God forbid you should call them old wives' tales.

During our endless Whatsapp chats leading up to my trip, many of them from the infamous taupe kitchen rubber floor, I had told her that I thought someone had poisoned the mind of the love of my life against me and persuaded him things couldn't change, convincing him to finally break away (people have a way of avenging their own past and misfortune on others, of hurting others, even if subconsciously, because they have been hurt). So, she arranged for her builder's elderly mother to perform the ritual of clearing the 'mau olhado' – the evil eye, who sends negative thoughts and energy to those he envies or is angry with. Open to anything and in a bit of a daze, I agreed. I had been brought up by a superstitious mother, who kept crystals in her bra, and a fado-singing grandmother, who sang songs of longing and yearning for a love lost as she hung up her bras, so was not fazed by the idea.

The next day, out of the bright Alentejo blue, a tiny lady appeared after lunch, sporting a black dress, her hair in a bun and a lifetime of wisdom in the wrinkles on her face. A picture seen on thousands of Portuguese postcards; women carrying baskets on their heads, while the men are sitting down, watching the world crawl by in the fifty-degree heat (as so wonderfully depicted in Ali Smith's accurate novel Alentejo Blue). Despite lunch being over, my friend's family were still hovering around curious, and in true English fashion, I began to feel awkward and crave privacy. Swiftly and sternly she shooed them away into the kitchen like local sheep into a pen, and reappeared holding a saucer of water. Without much introduction or small talk, the old biddy asked for some olive oil. Beside us the lunch table still showed clues to our delicious meal; red wine stains and crumbs from the crusty, yeasty typical sourdough loaf we had devoured with salty butter. As she reached over for the industrial-sized bottle of Portugal's finest extra virgin oil, a sense of comedy crept into my mind and added some much-needed light-heartedness to the scene. Before my eyes the spiritual and the mundane met in a hilarious juxtaposition of food and faith.

The clearing of the 'evil-eye' is apparently an ancient and widespread ritual in Portugal. It aims to bring an end to the effects of the negative energy that is being sent your way. This energy might just be negative thoughts or dislike, but could be stronger, coming from a place of envy, jealousy and anger, and wish you ill. How this energy affects you can vary, from physical pain to psychological anxiety, from financial problems, to marital. The clearing ritual is carried out to clear the bad energy and make space for higher vibrations, which will allow your life to start going better for you. Just what I needed.

And so it began. First the water was blessed with a prayer: "The Lord saw you, the Lord created you, may the Lord set you free from he who looked on you with an evil eye. In the name of the

Father, the Son and the Holy Spirit. Virgin of the Pranto remove this evil onlooker." Five drops of oil were allowed to fall from the bottle onto the water in the saucer and we – me, my friend, the wise biddy and her son – all looked on in silence, faintly aware of the busy bodies shuffling in the house just a few feet away, waiting eagerly for the prediction. The oil was expected to either join together to form one large circle, signifying that all was well, and no one meant me anything but good. Or to separate into individual drops and indicate that someone out there was sending unfriendly vibrations. We stared at the oil as it came together into a circle .... There was momentary relief. Then the circle shrank at the waist and drew apart, confirming my suspicions in two perfectly formed circles, brimming with bad wishes. While I pondered my predicament, the others chatted in a matter of fact way, as if I wasn't there. Then the old lady extracted her rosary from her black pocket and began to pray again, moving one bead at a time from her left hand to her right. Time after time she muttered the same prayer.

I remained silent. Still taking in the implications of the globules before me. Now what? Is there any reassurance in receiving a confirmation of your suspicions? A little, I guess. But an urge to shout out why me? What the hell did I ever do?!? Now as I look back, I feel sorry for anyone who has wished me unhappiness. If you have so little love in your heart from what you've seen as a child, that you can't find enough love to help those near and dear to you in times of need, then I'm much better off than you are. And I am much, much better off without these kinds of people in my life. Needing some time to take it all in, I retreated to my room to rest before part two later that day – a herb cleansing - hoping that the thick walls could keep out any further negative vibrations.

At dinner, trying to keep a clear head for what lay ahead, I stuck to just one glass of Alentejo white and ate lightly, as instructed. After supper I was led into the master bedroom, with its open plan bathroom. Asian silks in teal and light aqua hung behind the dark wood four poster bed and, feeling like a patient in care myself, I was oddly reminded that hospital cloaks are green to soothe patients' anxieties pre- and post- operation. On the polished cement sideboard, next to the carefully selected basins, there were lots of little clear plastic bags, brimming with herbs. Had I not known what was going on, I would have thought that they were growing weed, not eucalyptus, on the harmonious hill! My friend's sister, who was to perform the cleansing, entered and handed me a white soup bowl containing a pungent combo of herbs and told me to shower and rub them into my skin. As I stood in the glass enclosure, enjoying the sensation of the hot water blasting my shoulders, I suddenly felt as if I was seasoning a Sunday roast, as I rubbed the herbs into my sorrowful skin. All that was missing was garlic and lemon! Instead of lying on a bed of carrots and celery, I stepped out of the shower, wrapped myself in a white fluffy towel and stood in the middle of the incense-filled room on a rattan mat. I felt more like sushi wrapped in seaweed than Sunday roast now.

My healer wafted more incense around me like a bishop in a cathedral, chanting softly. By day she worked in a regular job for a regular company and I pondered how funny it was that people who seem so ordinary, can have these mystical secret sides. It would make excellent conversation at dinner parties – "So what do you do in your spare time?" "I perform spiritual cleansings and talk with the dead ...". What a conversation starter!

Once the smoke had settled and my skin, crusty with herbs, had dried, I was beckoned onto the patio outside. The clear sky above was pitch black and dotted with an incredible amount of tiny sparkling stars, more than I had ever seen. Like freckles on a face. The air was still and not a sound could be heard. I sat on the mat, my soft towel acting as a tent from my neck down, preserving the heat of my hot shower in my herby body. The smell of incense had been replaced with eucalyptus from the trees across the lake below. The chanting intensified and she began to gesticulate, urging spirits from another plane to show up. Her arms rose and fell gently, swinging from side to side, as she walked around me, until suddenly she announced "I have an old lady here. She's very angry." My heart began to race. A ghost was there, angry with me? Oh crap! Luckily she continued, slightly out of breath now, "She isn't angry with you." Phew. "She's angry with your mother. She's tried to get through to her but she's not listening, so she's using you" she clarified. Great. Just my luck.

She proceeded to describe the old lady in greater detail; small, thick set, big bosom, hair in a bun. I racked my brain to think who it might be. My dreams had recently been troubled by cross spirits and, relieved that I wasn't their target, I was keen to pinpoint who exactly was using me as a go-between. Plenty of women in my family had died. Could it be my mum's mum, who had died when I was sixteen, hurling me into a torrent of anger with the universe? But she was tiny at death, from years of suffering with leukaemia, and her hair by then was short and grey. Could it be my godmother, who had passed away the year before also from leukaemia? Before her illness, she had had a full fifties figure, reminding me of Elizabeth Taylor, constantly avoiding cake to try and slim down her curves. But she didn't wear her lovely Italian black hair in a bun. Then again hers too had turned to a grey veil – only her beautiful blue eyes had kept their piercing radiance right until the last moments. And in any case, she hadn't been an angry soul – in all my life I had never seen her angry. Sweet, cheeky, caring. Never angry, at least not in front of me. But as she had been my father's first wife before my mum, maybe there were things I didn't know about (my mother's closet was overcrowded with skeletons).

My healer insisted the spirit woman was angry because my mum wasn't looking after herself. She was being stubborn and ignoring the universe's attempts to get her to slow down and take care. This was true. An unfortunate fall seven years earlier had resulted in a broken hip. Anger at her misfortune had consumed her for years and prevented her from focussing on getting strong and moving on. Easily done. We're only human. Looking back now, it is easy for me to recognise that, had I not had the support described in this part of the book, the support needed to love myself, I too might have failed to focus on getting strong. I urge anyone struggling to let go of anger and seek help.

So, who else could the spirit be? Of course! Oma, my father's seemingly stern, German mother, who was understandably bitter at the Brits for razing her hometown of Bremen to the ground. She had certainly been stout and VERY bosomed. Did she wear her hair in a bun? Not that I had remembered but maybe. I had spent very little time with her in the seventeen years she was around. And she certainly had cause to be angry with mum; her son had married not one but two short, dark, Mediterranean women, rather than a tall, blond, Arian like his sister. I laughed as I recalled the last time I had visited her in Hamburg. Steffi and Boris had just won at Wimbledon. German pride and confidence, not lacking on any day, was sky high, atmospheric. We were sitting at the breakfast table eating traditional rye bread, ham and cheese. I had been missing my Sugar Puffs and crumpets with jam. Then it came out of the blue. A phrase that I would never have imagined from my grandmother, a person who is supposed to see only the wonder in her child's child. "Schade", (what a shame) she sighed over the strong, black, sweet coffee, typical in north Germany, "Your legs are so short and your bosom so small. Not like German girls." Stunned, I had paused, then pretended that my German was too rubbish to have understood. "Please may I have another piece of bread" I asked politely, thankful for the simple phrase learnt in school.

"I think it's my German granny" I told her back in the more useful, present moment and out of the bizarre, unhelpful past. "Tell her to go in peace. Tell her you forgive her and love her," she instructed calmly. Hesitant after years without speaking a single word of German, I embarked on a rusty conversation. I asked her kindly to leave and join her husband and son (my father, who sadly had passed seven years before his father) and pleaded with her to stop appearing in my dreams. Not entirely convinced that the figure had been correctly identified, I addressed her nonetheless, willing to try anything for peace and quiet. There under the stars, I chatted in a language I hadn't spoken in over ten years, with a woman I hadn't seen for over a quarter of a century. Surreal is putting it mildly. But gradually I felt her retreat. "She's gone" it was confirmed. And as I opened my eyes and looked up at the star-studded heavens above, I saw one momentarily get brighter … before fading then vanishing completely.

This roast was cooked. Exhausted. As the warm water in the shower fell on my shoulders once more and washed the ancient, traditional herbs away, I watched them circle at my feet before disappearing beneath the contemporary chrome drain. I didn't feel lighter or clearer as I had expected but something had shifted.

> There in the hidden paradise, something had revealed itself; something was beginning to come out of the shadows and into the light. And it was allowing me to feel and see the light, and the love, too.

There was one more step to take in this faithful cleansing journey towards self-love, before I was to go home to my ritual and spirit-free life in southwest London. During one of our daily trips to the local market, to buy fresh yeasty bread and locally fished bream and bass, my friend had driven me to the local village church to check out the times of the Masses. She had also taken the liberty to call the priest, whose name and number could be found on a heat-burnt, curled piece of paper on the old wooden door of the church. After a few rings a man answered and without hesitation agreed to include my dead relatives in his Mass. It was as simple as me ordering Papa John's pizza over the phone.

We turned up at seven. Having only ever been to church for weddings, funerals and school carol services, I was expecting a vaulted ceiling over dozens of heads, all ready for an evening of song and prayer. But we were led to a small side room. There were a few wooden benches and a simple altar. The priest welcomed us all and said a prayer. The theme that evening was about Mary Magdalen, who is said to have witnessed Jesus' crucifixion and resurrection. I felt as if my own demise was being laid to rest and my resurrection welcomed in. After his sermon the priest, without introduction, listed the people we were remembering and praying for that day. One by one he named my mother's mother, my great, great aunt, my grandfather and my uncle, all now on another plane. Alert after the soothing sermon, I was as worried that I had got some of their names wrong, as I was of being exposed as an imposter, only there to usurp others' longstanding faith. But those negative thoughts soon subsided and I was able to wish my rellies well too, before stepping back into the glaring orange light of the imminent sunset.

There in the remoteness of the village and slightly out of my comfort zone, I allowed myself to believe in the Universe in a way I hadn't before. No-one was trying to convert me or persuade me to align my beliefs with theirs. People, friends and strangers, were just offering me love and light. Nearly four years later, through my own growth and with help from 'believers' such as Jim Carey, Wayne Dyer, Jen Sincero and Christie Marie Sheldon, who have all helped me, I have come to see that the name you give your faith is irrelevant. For some it is God, or Allah, or Buddha, or Spirit, or Divine Source Energy or simply The Universe. The name is unimportant. What is important is that you understand that there is a universe we inhabit, a universe that is full of energy and light and love. Some of it is visible, which makes it easier to believe in, and other bits require unquestioning belief and faith. And we are a part of that universe. We need to acknowledge it, connect with it, relate to it and to our place in it. Once we have done that, and continue to do it, daily, we can feel the light, the love and the energy that is waiting there for us, and in us.

We don't need others to make us feel loved or strong.
But unless we realise that love is out there and in us, we
won't be able to use that power for our own happiness.

I was lucky then in a way, as I had friends who were willing to lend me their favourite self-help book, text me for months, offer me a place to retreat to, clean me of ill-willing low vibrations and energy-sapping spirits and drag me to churches filled with love. And I am forever grateful to those friends. But another thing I have come to learn is that luck doesn't really exist. Everything is out there waiting for you to grab it. You just need to let the Universe know you need it, be open to signs of offering and be willing to receive it. Although raised by a 'martyr', who suffered and still suffers in silence, I have never been the type of person to keep my woes to myself. Sure I have had evenings where I have kept myself and my tears within my four walls, shutting the world out. But for the most part I have sought help and solace from friends and loved ones. This has perhaps sometimes come across as winging or self-pity. But my aim has always been to understand why things have happened, and what I can do about them, so that I can move on. That is perhaps what stopped my depression from getting to the stage where it would keep me in bed, unable to care for myself or my children, unable to tick the box that would have led to drugs and clinics.

The Universe is there and ours for the co-making. The thing about asking for help is that whatever love the Universe shows and offers you, you will undoubtedly give back. If you are in a place of pain and suffering, you are unlikely to be able to help others, to bring love to them. So, in a way, it is our duty to show we love ourselves enough to ask the Universe for help and love sometimes, then to continue to love ourselves by taking the necessary steps to 'fix' ourselves, so that in turn we can be strong enough to help others. I guarantee that once you have been touched by the unconditional love that the Universe is waiting to give you, you will want to share it with others. Guaranteed.

So, if you are feeling low, reach out. Send that text. Write that email. Hey, be old-school and pick up the phone. Hang around for a chat in the playground. Go for coffee. Or for a drink. Book that haircut or massage. Talk to the hairdresser or the masseuse. Get someone to look after your dog or your kids for a few days and go away. Sign up for that course. Register at the online date site. No 'I shouldn't'. No 'I couldn't'. No 'what if' or 'if only'. Show the people around you and the Universe that you matter and watch what happens.

> As the Buddha said "You, yourself, as
> much as anybody in the entire universe,
> deserve your love and affection."

I have often been criticised for my actions – pursuing an ill-paid career I loved, leaving a well-paid job I hated to start my own business, moving my kids to Portugal so they could feel Portuguese, opening a shop and buying a house in a recession to try and lay roots abroad, moving my kids back to England to prevent total financial ruin, quitting work to retrain as a teacher at 41, taking the kids to see expensive plays, booking many a holiday on a credit card … and asking my husband to move out because he had made a life changing decision without me that made me feel worthless. But each of those actions I did out of love and a desire to grow. To take from life whatever I could. For me and for my children. For a variety of reasons some of the actions were less 'successful' than others, and I have made a point of learning from those.

In her fabulous book "You are a badass" Jen Sincero explains that to get the life you want, the life the Universe has in store for you, you have to do five things: know what you want, believe you can get it, connect with source, vibrate high energy and act. Looking back, I think I have mostly followed steps one, two and five. There was a little lack of belief here and there, some guilt, some shame, some inherited baggage. But there on that hill, in that village, on that five-day 'cleansing' break, I didn't just lose an evil onlooker and a sleep-disturbing spirit. I found the steps I had been missing. I saw others connect with 'source'. I felt others 'vibrate' the energy of love. I didn't even know I was seeing it, and without realising it I had started what was to become an amazing journey. One where, without a grand plan, other than to become abundantly happy, I would gently open up to and pursue any opportunity that I was presented with, always from a place of love not fear. And what a journey it has been.

Feeling clean and light, I returned to London to continue my journey. As my friend often said 'we crazies' do things slightly differently.

Step 3: Get guided! Let the stars show you the way.

As you can see by now, 2014 was a busy summer for me on my unplanned, unfolding, spiritual journey towards healing my broken heart. As well as encountering visible encouragement in the black and white comic words of Ruby's book, and experiencing quasi-palpable visits from beyond the grave, I was also offered less visible guidance in the shape of a reading of my astral chart. More specifically, a chart of my strengths and challenges for the period from January 2014 to December 2016. Until then I hadn't delved much into the world of astrology. Sure, along with my school friends, in the 80's we had spent mornings before register, sat on our wooden desks reading our horoscopes in Just Seventeen magazine, keen to get signs about the next snog at that weekend's party. And to pass the time on the dull commute to work in the 90's, I had been known to skip to the back of the Evening Standard and see what lay on the horizon for me and my fellow Librans. But I had never taken astrology too seriously. Until then.

In case some readers aren't 'au fait' with astrology, here is a quick 101 lesson. Astrology has been popular for many thousands of years. The Zodiac (apparently derived from the Greek word meaning "circle of animals") is believed to have developed in Ancient Egypt and was later adopted by the Babylonians (a people that lived in modern-day Iraq in the 18th BC).

According to some, astrology is 'the study of the movements and relative positions of celestial bodies, interpreted as having an influence on human affairs and the natural world'. By celestial bodies, they mean the planets in our solar system: the Sun, the Moon, Mercury, Venus (the love planet), Mars (the sex planet), Jupiter, Saturn, Uranus, Neptune and Pluto. Or as some put it rather more spiritually, it is "the search for human meaning in the sky". And who isn't searching for meaning, whether it can be found?

Over many generations, people have tried and tested the early teachings of astrology and found that it can provide powerful answers about the meaning and purpose of our life here on earth. According to astrology, your birth chart - a map of the planetary positions at the time and place of your birth – which can appear indecipherable at first, actually maps out different elements and how they fit together, to provide insights about every aspect of your personality. Basically, it explains why you do the things you do, when you do them.

As all seven billion of us are unique, so too are the factors that intertwine to form a complex portrait that is totally unique to YOU. As the father said to Patch in 101 Dalmatians, you are 'one of a kind', not one in 7,000,000,000! Time has a strong part to play in astrology, as the position of the planets and the energy they emit at that moment, define a 'moment in time'. Since we're part of the story of our Universe, our moment of birth and where the planets were at that time, is meaningful to us. The planets continue to move after our birth, but they do so in relation to the fixed-in-time energies of our original birth chart. The exact position of the planets in our chart will only be repeated every 26,000 years, so you can't get much more unique or personal than that. So, what your birth chart offers you, is a way of understanding your strengths or talents and the challenges you have or will face, so that you can make informed and successful decisions in all areas of your life. Who doesn't want some of that?

How often have you asked yourself why you find some things easier than others? Or why certain things that seem hard to explain have happened to you? Or why sometimes your actions are successful, and other times they aren't? There is a reason for everything. We aren't the third rock from the Sun without consequence. In my view, it's planetary team-work. Universal energy.

Still not convinced? Try staring up at a full moon and not feeling a sense of inspiration, awe and wonder. Don't you ever feel that something divine is looking down on you? That we are part of an almost incomprehensibly large expanse, and that there is an intimate aura around us? Some compare us to dancers at a ball (or disco, whatever you like to imagine), and what astrology offers us is a way of understanding our moves. Whether life feels like a rhythmic Waltz or a passionate Tango, or a frenzied Charleston, the patterns and relationships in our life can often be explained by those same patterns and relationships in our solar system. It is nothing more mystical than combining things we know or can see - the planets' positions, where and when we arrived in this universe, our relationships with others, the four elements (earth, water, air and fire) – as a tool to find something we can't always see: the meaning of our life.

Maybe you prefer to have a scientific, 'rational' outlook on life and the Universe and think that if it isn't a science, it isn't real? You are completely entitled to that. But perhaps like some you could open your mind to the view that astrology is a metaphysical science; beyond the physical, like other holistic and intuitive beliefs about energy patterns, such as feng shui (careful where you place your bed or your bin) acupuncture, yoga, reiki and tai-chi. Would it reassure you to know that astrology is the earliest known attempt to order our existence, long before man began recording history? Some would actually consider it a 'master science'!

Whether you feel compelled to get your chart read ASAP or are just reading on out of curiosity, hopefully like me, you see some sense in the above. For me it provided a useful tool on my path to healing and self-discovery.

The pieces of the puzzle may not seem to fit at first, but if you have faith, without trying to force things, at a certain point it "clicks" and the orchestrations of the cosmically-unfolding dance make sense.

If your life seems like a series of meaningless, sometimes un-related events, your astrological chart can be a comforting, reassuring sign that perhaps things happen for a reason. Sometimes it explains things that have already happened. Other times it forewarns of periods that will be challenging. The chart can also shine a light on your inner contradictions and point out natural strengths that you aren't taking advantage of as fully as you could or should. As a map of your psyche, your chart can be a guide to self-understanding, that never stops revealing new layers of insight, as you never stop growing and developing on your journey through life.

Coming back to the Zodiac, if I am one of a kind, I hear you protest, how can reading about all Librans in the back of the paper apply to so many of us? It is said that there is truth in stereotypes. The essence of each Zodiac sign's energy has built up a reputation over the millennia of astrological studies. Geminis are often said to be chatty, gossipy and have bright wit. This doesn't fit at all with a Gemini close to my heart, my mother, but as there are probably about sixty million other Geminis out there, I will just assume she is not your stereotypical Gemini (or your stereotypical anything for that matter). Scorpio is said to be sultry and intense. Again, that really doesn't fit with a Scorpio I spent twenty-one years with, but again he isn't your average bloke either, and most other Scorpios I know do fit that description perfectly! Finally, Virgos are said to be purist and neat-freaks and yet again a godmother to one of my three is open-minded, liberal and loves piles of things, so she too doesn't fit the mould. What is important is to hold those stereotypes loosely, as we make our own observations. What we are like depends on our birth-time-and-place determined planet, sign and house, so of course there will be exceptions to the rule.

So, assuming you see sense in the Universe giving off an energy that affects us down here on Earth, how can astrology help? Well, one way is with relationships. And in 2014 I was desperate to understand what had happened with mine. It can provide clues as to why you are attracted to, repelled by or indifferent to people you meet in life. It can help you take personality clashes less to heart when you encounter someone you really don't like at work or at a dinner party. It can also raise potential red flags to watch out for before an important event or coming together of different people. Some of the connections we make in life are sparked by friction, and rather than reject or walk away from anyone who riles us, astrology can help you take the long view, and see them as challenges that help both parties to grow. How I wish I had learnt that a decade ago …

Romantic relationships can benefit from a little bit of zodiac-sign wisdom too. In this day and age of screening our future partners online according to their filtered profile picture and carefully crafted blurb, astrology, with its millennia of studies, can fill you in on the dynamics of your potential future soulmate. In the delicate beginnings of a new liaison, it can shine a light on the behaviour of your new interest and either help you keep an open mind … or encourage you to follow your intuition and run a mile! Swipe left or right seems a little uninformed now, doesn't it?

So rather helpfully, astrology can give us – whether we are healing or just curious - a deeper understanding of all our relationships - with our boss, siblings, parents, children, friends or partners. Comparing a couple's birth charts alerts them to areas where their natures could come into conflict. It could be as useful as knowing how many children you want to have, whether you want to live in an urban or rural place, state versus private education. Known as "synastry," this can give you the heads-up about challenges that lie ahead, so that you can be forewarned and ready to support each other to fulfil your individual dreams or destinies. Marriage guidance from above, who'd say no to that, given that half of all marriages end in divorce, and almost 80% if one of you comes from a broken home!

And if you dare to follow astrology to its full depths, some say it shows where karma is being played out (think 'what goes around, comes around'), often with hard but necessary lessons being learnt, but also offers or predicts the potential for transformational miracles that may lie ahead .... And whether you believe it or not yet, transformation and miracles are closer and more frequent than you might think. Believe me. Or even better, ask my friends. They've seen my transformation. My mini-miracles. Thank you universe. Thank you planets and stars.

Enough about what astrology is. What did my chart say, I hear you shout? That is too personal even for this book and is for me to know. You go find out about yours – the guidance is priceless, trust me. What I will say however is that seeing in black and white when the stars and planets were aligned in my favour or not, with regards to work and house moves, as well as with regards to relationship love versus tension, explained so many moments of stress in my life from 2012-2014 and helped me shift from a place of self-blame and self-loathing, to a place of self-forgiveness and eventually self-love. Some of the mountains I had simply tried to climb at the wrong time. There is no point in thinking 'if only ...' but at least now I check whether the stars and planets are aligned in favour of my plans before I act, so that they can show me the best way. It isn't a question of changing my goals and reams, rather just knowing when to act on them for the best outcome.

Step 4: Get help! Explore traditional CBT, then turn to MBCT.

Being fully aware, as I was, that I was in a 'clean' and 'guided' but nonetheless bad place in September 2014, and fearful that it wouldn't pass alone despite Ruby's hints, I spoke to my lovely lady G.P. and asked for counselling. I was promptly sent a form in the post, which asked me to identify on a scale of 'not at all, several days, most days or always', various questions, to assess whether I was anxious or depressed. Whether my state of mind was preventing me from doing the daily things that are generally thought to show whether you are, or are not, ok. As I had never stopped being able to look after the kids or the house, on paper I was fine. But I was given an appointment with a CBT counsellor anyway.

In case you are unfamiliar with Cognitive Behaviour Therapy or CBT, it has been around for fifty years, since it was pioneered by the psychoanalyst Dr Aaron Beck, a psychiatrist at the University of Pennsylvania, who was testing concepts of depression and ended up with surprising findings. He discovered that depressed people have streams of negative thoughts which come up spontaneously – they have "automatic thoughts". These thoughts fall into 3 categories: about themselves, the world or the future (hence the questions in the assessment).

The trick is, when you are depressed you don't realise you are having these 'thoughts'; you think they are facts. So, Dr Beck came up with ways to help people identify and evaluate these 'thoughts', which led to patients thinking more realistically and consequently feeling better emotionally. As a result, they could function better too; their behaviour changed. Noticing their thoughts led to a change in actions. A long-term change. Genius (I have seen first hand as a Mindfulness-Based Cognitive Therapy teacher since 2016).

Since the '60's CBT has been explored in over a thousand studies and shown to have a positive effect treating many kinds of psychiatric, psychological and medical conditions, such as depression, anxiety, obsessive compulsive disorder (OCD), panic disorder, post-traumatic stress disorder (PTSD), phobias, eating disorders (such as anorexia and bulimia), sleep problems (such as insomnia) and problems relating to alcohol misuse. So, it was my turn to give it a go. I was so sad, that I was willing to try anything to take me back to a place where I could feel love, not fear.

I had tried counselling twice before, so should have known it was not for me, not in this shape and form anyway. Seven years earlier in 2007, just 8 weeks after our youngest daughter was born, while still breast feeding, I had suggested couples' therapy, as we were living in the same house, but with a chasm between us. I suspected I was suffering from post-natal depression too, but dismissed it as hormones and sadness about our crumbling marriage. Even getting up in the middle of the night to sit on the shower-room floor in uncontrollable tears (not heard by my sleeping husband just three metres away), hadn't been a strong enough sign that I was low, really low.

Anyway, that first time in 2007 we had been directed towards a therapist in Southfields. Having expressed milk and asked my mother to babysit the three children under six, we drove the 5 minutes down Merton Road in an oddly unified silence. There was a fragile sense in the air that we wanted this to work and were optimistic about the outcome. On arrival we were beckoned into a cosy front room and the questions started. I cannot remember how we got onto the topic of my father's suicide when I was two quite so quickly, but I do remember her stating firmly, what felt like out of nowhere, that I clearly had abandonment issues. What the hell! I remember thinking. We are here to talk about why my husband disappears until 5am once a month having said he is on the way home at 7pm, and fails to turn up for date night, leaving me alone on the sofa watching Trinny and Susanna with a 2-month-old, M&S meal for two burning in the oven, and the most pressing thing you have to tell me is that I have abandonment issues! Too effing right, if it means I am hurt by being abandoned on a Friday night to care for OUR third child alone. But what does that have to do with a guy who killed himself 35 years earlier …. (Now in my calm, grounded, psychology A Level-informed state, I know exactly what it has to do with it, but then I was not in the right place to explore it, and she should have seen that.)

From that moment, my rage shut my ears and I was keen to leave. Oddly my despair and confusion brought us together momentarily, as he too agreed that it wasn't quite the approach we had hoped for. I didn't go near CBT for another seven years. Sadly, now I know she was right. But the timing and tone had been completely wrong. As a Mindfulness Based Cognitive Therapy teacher myself now (isn't it amazing how things change in our universe?), I respect my participants' path, their readiness … I hold them in a place of love and care. I guide them to name insights that can help them grow and be happy. That experience felt like I had been hit by a wrecking ball ...

My second experience of counselling had been a bit less violent (just). It was in 2010. I had been recommended to approach a well-known counselling charity for help with our crumbling marriage, after he decided to stay abroad and leave me to raise the three children alone in the UK. Despite actions that signalled the opposite, I was sure he didn't really want to end the eighteen-year relationship (he had told me so himself and I was pretty good at being attached to us then), so I rang and got an appointment in nearby Wimbledon. This time the room at the centre was cold and clinical. Like the previous lady, the counsellor was grey haired, appeared gentle, and was in her late middle age. It was a Monday during one of his fortnightly visits to the UK and he was due to fly back later that night. We had one hour for £60. No pressure. I just wanted to get answers as to why he was doing what he was doing. After clarifying that to the counsellor, she started to ask a series of questions: how were our intimacy needs being met, what was communication like. Then somehow, and I am still baffled as to how, he got onto the topic of the state of the civil engineering employment market and he was off. No more mention of our marriage, our family, our separated state, no more mention of us at all. And she made no (effective) attempt to rein him back in. Forty-five minutes later we had a very clear idea of how hard jobs were in the current climate in engineering, but not a clue how to save our marriage.

I was incensed, partly because of the money and time lost, but mainly because he had been allowed to dodge the issue ... again. Even employing a so-called expert and putting him on the spot had failed to get him to talk about US. The drive home up Wimbledon Hill was tense. It would have been easier to push the car up the hill, than get him to look inside himself and share. So, as a gesture of love for myself, I put an end to the counselling, explaining that I had two weeks alone with the kids ahead of me and didn't need to get into this state of frustration every fortnight, only to be left alone. My sanity to care for the kids was all that I cared about. My faith in counsellors and therapy was, for a second time destroyed.

So, four years later, now an official single mother, and struggling with the reality of my life partner having moved on with someone else, I found myself so low, that I was willing to dismiss the first two disastrous encounters with therapy and turned up at the GP's practice. The room allocated to CBT sessions was more of a broom cupboard-come-office. I was invited to sit in a low chair opposite the dark-haired, steely-faced lady in her late thirties/early forties. I felt sick in my stomach and my eyes were tired from crying earlier that day. I felt totally vulnerable and helpless. She asked me to explain why I was there and her first, her FIRST, comment was to tell me that I clearly had an issue letting go. My numb state prevented me from feeling winded, just dazed. Slightly slapped in the face, rather than punched in the stomach as before.

But even in my low place, I had a strong sense of how I deserved to be 'treated' and this wasn't it.

I suggested that her approach was a little presumptuous or hasty. But she was having none of it. She dug her heels in and I put up my wall. I left the surgery vowing NEVER, not ever, to go near traditional CBT again.

Now if you have had an experience similar to mine, my heart, and a massive hug, goes out to you. When we admit our vulnerability, and ask for help to love ourselves and/or others, we deserve compassion and kindness back. Not cotton wool but not a bulldozer either. Luckily I have since then become a Mindfulness Based Cognitive Therapy trainer myself and know CBT can work, but it needs to be done properly. With compassion. The hard truth can be made visible gently.

Done well, CBT can achieve great things. It can change lives. Done well, it can help you realise that your thoughts IN THIS MOMENT, feelings IN THIS MOMENT, physical sensations IN THIS MOMENT and consequent ACTUAL actions or urges are all interconnected, and that unnoticed negative thoughts and feelings can trap you in a vicious cycle, leading to low mood. Once you show up for CBT you have taken the hardest step; to love yourself enough to do something that will help you get happy. When life seems overwhelming, mindful, compassionate CBT can help you notice negative patterns and deal with them in a positive way. The focus is always on NOW, not on the past. What I was subjected to were issues from a two-year-old me. Also relevant and useful, but not what I had asked for or needed in the miserable state I was in at forty four. That retrospective would come later.

So, if you want to understand how awareness of your thoughts can lead to actions of self-love, try CBT. But make sure you find a compassionate therapist. Not one who appears to be using you as a case study for some Freudian theory. Just google MBCT near you (or email me) and you will find someone who will give you the tools to be your own saving grace, daily, moment by moment. With the Universe by your side. Your therapist should ask you to state your CURRENT thoughts, feelings and sensations. Not ask you for a summary of your life and promptly put you in a psychobabble box – abandonment and attachment issues. MBCT is about life skills to help you live a happy, joyous and peaceful life. We all have aversion or attachment to things in our lives, but we can be expertly and skilfully guided to realise that. Empowered to own that. Not be gunned down by others' 'professional' opinion and textbook labels.

So, as the title of this chapter suggests, to learn to love yourself, do get help. But make sure it is good and offered by someone who has the ability to start with focussing on what is happening now, not 35 years ago, the ability to stay on track analysing thoughts and feelings about why you showed up, not external factors about employment economics.

> *Choose someone who is able to guide you gently, kindly,*
> *at a speed that suits your capacity to change yourself.*

Don't try to solve problems in the wider world, just focus on your challenging thoughts and feelings, one step at a time, one breath at a time. Once you are skilled to deal with THIS MOMENT, sure, explore underlying issues such as an early bereavement or an unhappy childhood. But start by loving your you of TODAY first. Start with Mindfulness.

Step 5: Get loved ... it really is 'all around'!

One of the first things I tell my audience when I am giving an introductory presentation about Mindfulness, is that it is secular. We (Mindfulness teachers) are compelled to mention a lack of religiousness or Buddhism, to make it accessible to people of all faiths. Religion has become so stigmatised by 9:11, that there appears to be a suspicion of all things religious. One Catholic audience member of mine even told me she thought Mindfulness contradicted her faith, as it invites us to turn to our breath in moments of worry, whereas she wanted her daughter to turn to God. Luckily on that occasion I didn't have to explain how wrong she was, as we were assured by a Catholic nun in the audience that one does not exclude the other. That we are more connected to our faith with our breath. That God or the Universe, is our breath. Thank you, Sister.

Personally, I have never been naturally pro-religion anyway, as my mother had shunned her Catholic roots before I was born. I was raised not to believe in the Church or a God (I am leaving the story of why my mother might believe we are living in a Godless universe for my next book.) By the age of ten I had opted-out of saying the Lord's Prayer at Primary school (yet 37 years later I can still recite it and take great delight in showing this to my kids who attend C of E schools and can't!). Churches in my life were for weddings and funerals. And my own wedding had taken place in Chelsea Town Hall. So the last place I expected to learn to love myself and find love, salvation even, was in a church.

It all started on a lonely kid-free weekend soon after the end of the summer holidays that summer, 2014. I had been so uplifted by the mass in the Alentejo for my absent male family members (as guided by the stars on THAT hill), that I decided to ask for one for my three absent grandmothers (my mother had a biological mother and a nurturing mother). Maybe my lack of peace stemmed from them needing some attention too, I wondered?

So I emailed the vicar at the church where my kids' school sang carols every year. He was a parent in my youngest's class, so it felt a bit awkward but as he was technically on sabbatical at the time, his substitute replied. When you ask the Universe for help it knows you are listening and will offer you help on your path to healing. Not only did the sub-Vicar agree to mentioning and praying for my family in the next Eucharist service, but she also put it out there, that there were opportunities for me too. I was offered a 'confidential conversation' with her and an option for a Sacrament of Reconciliation (the protestant version of Catholic Confession). I could also attend a special service that included anointing with oil and the laying of hands, for my wholeness and healing. Although I had felt totally at ease receiving help with ritualistic oil and spiritual hands on the hill in the Alentejo, somehow the idea of receiving similar from a person of the cloth, did not seem as easy to accept. I felt like an imposter. Picking and choosing support from a faith on my terms, to suit me. So I set a date to attend a service and have a conversation, but nothing more. Today I would be more than happy to hold hands with people of any religion, as I know we are all being looked after by the same Universe, just under a different brand.

The service was at 11am the day before my 44th birthday and immediately after a yoga lesson in the same church. My mind was ready to receive. Love, guidance, anything the Universe had to offer. As I walked down the church to the small area at the front right where a circle of chairs was laid out, my feelings of intrusion and taking advantage of others reappeared. But as soon as I saw the kind faces of the others attending the intimate service, that all melted away. There was no suspicion in their eyes, no one was questioning my right to be there. Those were just thoughts in my head. Fiction. I sat among them and listened and slowly softened to the faith that was palpable. The Reverend celebrated the Eucharist and mentioned my three dead grannies, in my attempt to appease whoever had turned up in anger on the hill. With so many skeletons in my mother's closet, it was like a shot in the dark for me, but I was willing to try anything to give them peace, so that I might get some in return.

After the service there was tea and biscuits. Nobody questioned my presence or asked intrusive questions. Half of me wanted to leave this place where I felt far from at home, but the other half was enjoying the kindness and company. It can be lonely in your head. So, I sipped and munched and slowly softened.

By the time I left I was light and warm. Nothing in particular had been said or done. But I had been received, loved and held. The Universe had offered me that in the least expected of places. Having always appreciated churches for their architectural beauty, I now had another level of appreciation for them.

It was another two weeks before I could have my confidential conversation at 5.30pm on a Sunday evening. I made sure the kids would be returned by their father a little later than usual. I was nervous as I parked. I had no idea what the Reverend could possibly say or do that would alleviate my sense of sadness and loneliness but I was hopeful after the warm welcome a fortnight earlier. There was no sensation of being a 'user' or imposter this time. Just a sad soul needing some helpful words from the Universe.

The room, just off the Reverend's 'office' was long and thin, neither warm nor austere. I can't remember who started talking or how. But I do recall the Reverend's face, as she listened without judgement. I guess I told her about our four-year separation after eighteen years together, with three aborted attempts in three years to get back together, those three further blows to an already broken heart. About taking my stress of being bullied at work and of my frustration of his lack of action to save us, out on him at Christmas the year before, which had been the straw that had broken the camel's back. The news four months earlier that he had met someone else at the beginning of the year but kept it secret for six months, and announced it on the worst day of my medical life, before blurting it out to the kids, as one lay naked in the bath aged ten, on the eve of our oldest's 13th birthday, leaving me to hold her as she cried herself to sleep in my arms for two nights in a row. About how I had a dark cloud hanging over me that had made me leave my job in July after crying in front of my Year Three pupils. Crying that had lasted 120 days. And she just listened, reassured, allowed, encouraged, held my aching heart in her attention unconditionally.

I wasn't labelled as abandoned or attached. I was given permission to feel hurt. To ache. Permission not to worry about what would happen to my kids now that they were being raised by a teary, single mum. The one thing I had wanted to avoid all my adult life. The one thing that was out of my control. I was given permission not to be responsible for everything and everyone.

A box of tissues and sixty minutes later I was told to just be kind to myself. Nothing else mattered. There was nowhere else to start. Not with him or them. With me. Those were the only words I needed to hear. No labels. Just confirmation that I was loved and love was all around. And permission to love and heal myself. Thank you, Reverend.

And that is exactly what I did. And haven't stopped doing. When you start by loving yourself, everything else falls into place.

Here's how I did it. How I made the shift. A google, a call, a drive and 8 short weeks on the path to self-love. To happiness, joy and peace. One mindful breath at a time …

Part two: LEARN TO LIVE IN THIS MOMENT

Step 6: Get Mindful; wherever you go, here you are.

Before I share how I learnt these transformative life skills, a few words about what Mindfulness is, as it is greatly misunderstood by many.

The Buddha said "Do not dwell in the past, do not dream of the future, concentrate the mind on the present moment." That is the underlying concept of Mindfulness, which I had been introduced to, as I lay in the sun that summer in 2014, holding on for dear life to a past that was no longer, and dreaming of a future when I would wake up and it would have all been a bad dream. It is a concept that Jon Kabat-Zinn took the Buddhism out of and made his own for his patients back in the 70's, with his definition that "Mindfulness is the awareness that arises through paying attention, on purpose, in the present moment, non-judgementally." Words that would literally save my life. They could save yours.

Before going any further, I have to make it very clear that neither Jon Kabat-Zinn nor Mindfulness are Buddhist. In fact, Kabat-Zinn was born Jewish. However, as he was growing up his beliefs became a coming together of science and art. While he was a student at MIT he was introduced to meditation by a Zen missionary called Philip Kapleau. And there is no denying that Kabat-Zinn did train in Buddhist principles, including studying meditation with Buddhist teachers such as Thich Nhat Hahn (who passed in January 2022) and the Insight Meditation Society, where he later taught. But as far as I know, he himself does not identify as a Buddhist. Recently (before the pandemic) he travelled around the world working with organisations and governments to help them see beyond their fears. I was lucky enough to meet him at the 2018 Mindfulness in Schools Project conference, where he talked about the future of Mindfulness in education and so accurately described mindful meditation as allowing each and every one of us to have 'a love affair with our sanity and beauty'.

In 1979, when I was just nine years old and happily playing in the gardens of our Putney Heath council flat, 3300 miles away, Kabat-Zinn founded the Stress Reduction Clinic at the University of Massachusetts Medical School. There he adapted the Buddhist teachings on Mindfulness that he had received, and developed the first eight-week Stress Reduction and Relaxation Programme. Soon however the Buddhist framework he had used was removed, and as I've said, any connection between Mindfulness and Buddhism was completely toned down. The revamped and clearly secular MBSR as it is still known today (Mindfulness-based Stress Reduction) was rolled out at the newly founded Center for Mindfulness in Medicine, Health Care and Society at the University of Massachusetts Medical School with one aim; to help patients suffering with stress, pain and illness cope. To breathe. To live.

If, unlike me, you are the kind of person who needs reams of empirical evidence before you consider trying something, you will be pleased to know that for the next two decades Kabat-Zinn's research focussed on exploring mind and body connections, for the purpose of healing his patients. He explored the effects of MBSR on the brain and how it processes emotions, particularly under stress, and on the immune system. How many of us have gone through a period of cold after cold, or had a long cold that just wouldn't shift, and failed to identify that it coincided with a period of stress in our lives? Jon Kabat-Zinn even investigated the use and effects of MBSR on women with breast cancer and men with prostate cancer, as well as on patients receiving bone marrow transplant. His work was carried out with a variety of groups, from prisons to corporations. And until 2015 Kabat-Zinn was part of a group called the Mind and Life Institute, that organised events with the Dalai Lama and scientists from the West, in order to encourage greater understanding of the nature of the human mind and our emotions. There is no doubt that Mindfulness was raised by a scientific family, not a religious one. And I am grateful to them for their hard work. Jon Kabat Zinn said in 2018 that the point of MBSR is to "befriend your mind to know what will cause suffering or harm' so that you can 'heal wounds by recognising they are here and that's ok'.

Sound useful? It was for me.

Ruby's journey to Mindfulness is worth noting here too. Back in 2011, after her career in acting and comedy ended 'with a bang', and having tried and failed to beat depression with medication and therapists, she was able to find a new remedy in the shape of a Masters in Mindfulness at Oxford (initiated by Mark Williams and Willem Kuyken). Thanks to Mark Williams and his colleagues, Jon Kabat-Zinn's MBSR work made its way across the big pond. Working on the treatment of depression and suicidal behaviour, Williams, Teasdale and Segal integrated key elements of cognitive therapy with the MBSR and developed the MBCT – Mindfulness Based Cognitive Therapy for the prevention of relapse in depression. Since then, studies have proven that MBCT reduces the recurrence rate in patients who have suffered three or more episodes of major depression as effectively as antidepressants. Imagine that – paying attention to your breath, relating to your thoughts in a non-emotional way, is actually as effective as taking a pill! I know which I would rather be dependent on. And the icing on the cake; the MBCT programme has been recognised by the UK National Institute for Clinical Excellence (NICE), as a main treatment for prevention relapse in depression. Your GP can prescribe a course of Mindfulness to you, rather than a jar of pills. Finally, as well as depression, in the UK MBCT is also being used with conditions such as chronic pain, psoriasis, cancer, anxiety, chronic fatigue, stress, psychosis and bipolar disorder. Not bad for something that many were willing to dismiss as Eastern dogma forty years ago. This 2500-year-old Buddhism-inspired approach is now globally recognised as an 'innovative' approach to helping mental health. Don't just take my word for it, try it!

So hopefully that has made it clear, that Mindfulness is neither Buddhist nor a fad. It can help across all faiths and is here in the West to stay. I have been teaching Mindfulness in secular and religious schools alike, with pupils from not just lay or Christian families, but Jewish, Sikh and Muslim too. Mindfulness encourages awareness of our thoughts and invites us to turn to our breath to remain present. In the Catholic faith, St. John of Damascus, defined prayer as "...the raising of one's mind and heart to God or the requesting of good things from God". How can you raise your mind to God if it is busy dwelling in the past or anxious about the future? Conversations I have had with a Catholic nun at one of my schools, have shown me an open-minded approach to understanding that Mindfulness can help people in prayer, not incite them to turn them away from God. Another Catholic Head Teacher I spoke with was completely un-phased when I warned him that some parents had shown concern about a clash between Mindfulness and Catholicism. He replied simply by saying "but God IS our breath" and continued to plan the courses.

Like the nun and the head teacher I am not threatened by any religious dogma that may or may not be attached to Mindfulness. Anyone who knows anything about Buddhism, knows that lack of dogma is actually one of its pillars. Sure, 2500 years ago the Buddha did travel throughout India for forty-five years spreading his teachings, but he did so helping everyone on the way, stealing no food and sleeping only where he could. He wasn't trying to convert. The same can't be said about some extreme Jesuits, who travelled throughout the world slightly more bullishly, in an attempt to convert as many people as possible to Christianity. Were they acting out of love of God or fear of other religions? Don't know, I wasn't there and I am not an historian. And this is not the place for religious debate. But I just wanted to clarify that Mindfulness is not a subversive attempt to convert people to Buddhism.

That said, by learning about how Mindfulness isn't Buddhist, in order to reassure the odd sceptical or fearful parent, I have learnt so much about Buddhism, that I sometimes play with the idea of converting myself (from what? I am non-religious). Buddhism is merely a non-dogmatic, non-violent suggested path of practice and spiritual growth to help individuals gain insight into the true nature of reality.

The practices offer a way of gaining clarity so that we can develop the qualities of awareness, kindness, and wisdom.

Who wouldn't want that? In the opinion of many, no other religion compares in what it offers: a full and natural way of life, harming the planet as little as possible, culminating in the end of suffering, in Enlightenment. And when I went online in September 2014 and signed up for my MBSR course, there was nothing I wanted to end more ... my suffering.

But there is more to Buddhism than Enlightenment, just like there is more to Mindfulness than awareness and breathing. To me personally, and not just as a Mindfulness teacher, Jon Kabat-Zinn kept some great bits derived from Buddhism in his course. Both support the idea that nothing is fixed or permanent and that the only truth is the moment we have right now. That was a fabulous promise to me in 2014, when I needed to hear that my state of sadness didn't have to be permanent. Both believe that change is possible, and I really needed things to change. After 120 days of tears I just wanted them to stop.

So how does it work, I hear you ask? Mindfulness suggests that changing from a state of low mood or anxiety is possible with a change of mind-set; a shift from obsessing about the past or future, to focussing on the present. A shift from looking for the negative or bad (even without meaning to, we are built that way to survive), to looking for the positive and the good. Buddhism suggests that actions have consequences. Science, close to Kabat-Zinn's heart, has proven cause and effect. Mindfulness suggests, and has actually scientifically been proven through the use of MRIs, that a shift in thinking in the way mentioned above, results in the creation of a new way of thinking, in neurological change. By training our brain to pay attention to this breath, this moment, and focus on the good, we actually create new neuron pathways in our brain that make us naturally more present and better positive thinkers over time. We train ourselves out of old habits and create new ones. Our half-empty glass gets fuller, just by paying attention and thinking positively! Don't you just love neuro-plasticity?

Maybe if the book I had found on the shelf in the Algarve in 2014 had been the Buddha's Dharma, I would be in Asia now studying meditation, rather than in England having taught Mindfulness to 6000 people. Who knows. But being open to new experiences and ways of thinking (kindly presented to me by the Universe), is what helped me wake up out of my sad, tearful stupor.

The word 'Buddha' is a title which means 'one who is awake', woken up to reality, able to understand life in the deepest way. And that is what Mindfulness did for me on that eight-week MBSR course – through lying down and sitting still, week after week, I woke up.

Now, I don't claim to understand everything, not after 8 years of practice, but I do know that through Mindfulness I was able to wake up to the notion that I could control my thoughts, not them me. That I could see life's harshness as the Buddha did – my father's suicide, our poorer years on the council estate, the end of my marriage, my mother growing old and ill, my godmother sick and eventually passing – without allowing those realities to cause me suffering. Pain, yes, but not suffering. Unlike the Buddha, I didn't start my journey seeking to know the truth about life and death, just seeking a day without tears.

But what I found on the Mindfulness course, as well as on other, consequent steps of my journey, was that, like the Buddha, if I looked into my heart and my mind and trusted my intuition, learning from all my direct present-moment experiences, I would become, in my own twenty-first century way, at the ripe old age of forty-four, in a room in southwest London, enlightened.

So I sat on a chair, not under a tree but in a room in SW4 with eleven other people and promised myself to practice for thirty to forty minutes each day, so that I could see the light at the end of my dark, tissue-littered, tear-drenched tunnel. Like the Buddha, I took forty days (well forty-three actually over the eight-week course) but I got there. I have no idea whether he faltered or 'cheated'. I know I did. Some days I fell asleep during a body scan. Or practiced on the treadmill, paying attention to my body as it ran on the rubber mat, getting nowhere, while my mind tried to get itself out of a rut. But as Mindfulness taught me and I now teach my students, self-compassion, self-love is the key. Better to stay awake for half a body scan or pay attention to your breath and your body while running rather than sitting still, than not at all.

With my Mindfulness teacher's expert and kind help, and the support of the other eleven participants, some of whom became friends, like the Buddha, I was able to reach a new, unconditioned place. One where my upbringing and my values, opinions and perceptions, could be 'watched' by me as a neutral observer. I was able to understand what had been causing my suffering. This new-found awareness or wisdom, driven by self-love and self-compassion, resulted in me losing my chains of negative rumination. Like the Buddha, I had achieved the goal of my quest. I was tear-free. Two weeks into the course, the daily crying came to a sudden halt. Sure there was the odd low point here and there (mostly at a certain time of the month when hormones challenged my Mindfulness). But by Christmas my monsoon had passed. The dry season had arrived.

So, having found Ruby on the shelf, my Mindfulness teacher, Tessa Watt, on the internet, and my breath in SW4, I travelled my eight-week journey to finding ME. I try really hard not to be evangelical about it (despite the previous pages that might look like I am). When people ask me what I do I tell them. If they seem keen to understand more, I tell them more. I usually start by saying Mindfulness is a sort of non-religious meditation. That loses some people. So, in case you are wondering, although one of the key premises of Mindfulness is 'suspend expectation', this is what you can expect on the eight-week MBSR and what I experienced. By the end of this chapter, I hope you will be googling where to find a course near you, as Ruby's experience led me to do (or emailing me to sign up onto one of mine!).

Week One is about awareness and automatic-pilot. We can go through life, from the minute we wake up until the minute we fall asleep, entirely "on automatic pilot"; almost completely and unknowingly unaware of what we are actually doing as we are doing it, moment-by-moment. You hear phrases such as having 'your head in the clouds' (often used about my son and his apparent 'day-dreaming', when actually he is taking the time to process what he has seen or heard, at his pace, mindfully) or being 'away with the fairies' or being 'miles away'. What they actually mean is that our attention is in our thoughts of the past or the future, effectively miles away from the present. From this moment.

What does this feel like? Ever found yourself in a conversation with someone and then they ask you a question that you can't answer, which is when you realise you had stopped paying attention and were lost in thought? Ever gone upstairs for something, only to get to the top of the stairs and not remember what you came for? Ever got to your destination by foot, train or car, only to realise you had literally switched off for a huge chunk of the trip?

For some things it is useful to be on autopilot – riding a bike, driving a car, swimming. But unfortunately for everything else it can be counter-productive, since on auto-pilot we are more likely to react thoughtlessly, rather than respond thoughtfully. Our mental distance from events happening around us and our lack of consciousness of our thoughts or feelings, can result in us snapping, lashing out, letting our buttons be pressed. Or having a go at someone for buying cheap profiteroles ... It isn't so much that we have a short fuse because we are Mediterranean, or a bad temper because we have red hair. Those are (mostly) myths. We just don't give ourselves the chance to notice the 'fuse wire' at all. On the teen MiSP dot.b courses I trained in, Mindfulness is 'sold' to teens as a way of giving them possibilities and choices. But it isn't just a selling-tool for teenagers. It works to 'persuade' adults too. By becoming aware of our thoughts and related feelings, we can all, young or old, gain the choice, the freedom to act, not react. We become free and full of possibility.

In addition to presenting the idea of auto-pilot as unhelpful, the first week looks at how to increase your awareness, your attention. With children aged seven to eleven on the MiSP paws.b programme, we joke that you never see an 'attention' lesson on the timetable for the day. But it's true. In the West we are never taught to pay attention. To concentrate. And certainly not in this day and age of rushing and filling every moment of the day with 'doing'. So we start to learn about paying attention. I don't want to give the game away too much, as I'd like you to discover things for yourself, but suffice to say that with the first practice you will become acutely aware of a member of the dried fruit family like you never knew you could. With each of the five senses, we practice using our attention on it, becoming more aware of it. Appreciating it. With beginners' minds. On that day in October 2014 I was amazed to see a lady in her sixties, who had a considerable dislike for this particular dried fruit discover, by really suspending expectation and ignoring what she already thought she knew (harder than it sounds), and replacing that with paying attention to what she could see, feel, smell, hear and taste in THAT moment, make an amazing discovery – she didn't dislike them after all. That is the power of awareness. When we do things on autopilot, like we have done them a million times before, we miss out on the here and now. On this vision, this feeling, this smell, this sound and in her case, this taste. Imagine going your whole life avoiding something because you were attached to a thought, a memory that you didn't like it, only to discover that actually you do! Mindfulness = not missing out.

The second exercise in awareness on that first session is called the Body Scan. Now don't be alarmed. There are no machines, no lasers. Just your own attention. As the aim of the programme is to increase awareness, we start by learning to become aware of our bodies. Handy, because like our breath, our other best friend, it is always with us, ready to tell us how we are feeling should we stop to ask it. Bit by bit we pay attention to our whole body, resting for a while on one part, like an anchor helping a boat rest at sea, such as a toe, a calf, a knee, before deliberately moving the focus of our attention to another part, breaking the habit of dwelling on one thing, time and time again, until we have 'scanned' our whole body. It is so beautifully simple yet so wonderfully powerful. And hopefully you don't fall asleep for all of it!

And part of that power comes from what we discover as we scan our bodies. Every thought can provoke an emotion, which in turn can provoke a body sensation. Ever wondered why your lower back hurts or your neck and shoulders are stiff? It isn't (just) old age! Or why you have a headache even though you have your mid-life reading glasses on and haven't been at the PC reading streams of emails or doing a mammoth food shop? Our minds and our bodies are inextricably connected. Stressful thoughts can trigger discomfort and even pain anywhere in our body. In fact, how pain shows up in our body still baffles doctors. But most of the time we don't even realise that that pain, those 'stress signatures' are there, desperately trying to get through to you, but only falling on deaf ears? The body scan is forty minutes of pure, unadulterated (except by the odd pesky thought) attention on your body. Indulging it with your purposeful attention, allowing it to be heard. On paws.b we use the imagery of a torchlight to help kids sustain their attention. On the dot.b we encourage teens to adopt a 'David Attenborough' attitude of curiosity. Anything to help participants explore and investigate sensations in their bodies, and just accept what they find without analysing or judging it. Just allowing it to be. Allowing it to tell you how you are. Like Chris Martin sang in the Coldplay song released that same year, it's 'Magic'. In half the time it takes to roast a chicken. Bargain.

In between week one and week two, there are three pieces of 'home practice' (as a teacher I am tempted to say homework). The first involves finding a time and a place every day to do a body scan for thirty to forty minutes with the assistance of an audio recording to guide you. The second involves choosing one routine activity that you do every day (brush your teeth, have a shower, make a cup of tea) and make a conscious effort to bring presence to it, moment by moment, a bit like a Japanese tea making ritual. Finally, you are invited to apply what you learnt eating the piece of dried fruit in the way mentioned above, to one meal a day. Not too taxing but often tricky, as you are likely to be stressed or low … given that that is what the course is designed to help with. So, it can feel hard to start.

Mindfulness and the MBSR are about breaking old habits and making new ones in order to make new pathways in the brain, and old habits as the saying goes, die hard. Or at least they can show some resistance. And resistance is what many find in that first week. But as Jen Sincero so aptly puts it in her 'Badass' series, we are trying to grow, trying to create a new us, and the old us, our ego, might show up and put up a bit of a fight. The key is not to struggle. Not to fight with this ego. Not to judge ourselves for falling asleep mid body scan. Not to criticise ourselves for finding it uncomfortable. Just to observe that first week. To accept any feelings of frustration. To allow things to be as we find them. And to breathe.

Week two, like the seventies and eighties New York band, is about living in our 'talking heads'. Imagine a black-robed 'judge' sitting in your head, and your every word and action, and those of the people in your life, sitting in the stand, being scrutinised, analysed and condemned, all day long. Loaded with expectations, we judge things as not good enough or not wanted. Clearly this habit of constantly comparing and judging is not a good influence on our life; it removes us from the present moment and denies us of the ability to see things as they are, as we focus on how we would like them to be. And so it denies us of the ability to live things as they really are. To miss out on many good things just because they don't compare with an imagined reality, with a preconceived expectation.

I was once teaching a class of ten to twelve-year olds. We were talking about how, if we have expectations, we are likely to identify gaps when we judge that reality is less than that expectation. One boy said he has learnt to go into every situation in life with no or very low expectations, so that reality can only be better. He has programmed himself to expect the worst. To prepare for the negative. I explained this to him and the class; heads tilted in contemplation and some eyes widened in the realisation of what this meant. "What if, you went into things with no expectation?" I offered as an alternative. Light bulbs lit up across the room in the heads of those who had understood the possibilities that this new outlook would offer.

Another of the pitfalls of living from a place of thinking and judging is that it is all too easy to fall into the habit of apportioning blame. By blaming situations or people we deny ourselves the freedom to act. We give away our freedom by saying things happened to us because of this or that. What if we just saw them and said, they happened? Then got out of our heads and into our senses, ready for the next event. And if we have this calm, present approach, we are more likely to be able to remember it (with our Hippocampus part of our brain) and not repeat the situation in the future. To learn. To grow. And every human on this planet has an innate desire to grow.

In week two we continue to use the Body Scan as a way of getting out of our heads and into our bodies. We learn to look at the sensations in our body as they are. Without overthinking. Without judging. Simply receiving what we found with kindness. Without any expectation or goal. We weren't even trying to relax. Just to be aware. To be. (Hopefully awake for longer than in week one.)

And even though by now some people had done seven body scans, since the beginning of the course, from the sounds that could be heard as we all lay there on the big orange cushions, with our feet falling to the side and our palms facing upwards towards the vaulted ceiling, some of us had fallen asleep. Some deep asleep from the snores that could be heard. Some just dropping in and out of consciousness. And that's ok. Everyone in the room had a different reason for being there but we all had one thing in common; an element of stress in one or more aspects of our life was causing us anxiety, preventing us from being truly happy. And living in that place is exhausting for the mind and the body. So, as you start practicing the Body Scan it is normal to fall asleep – the body twigs that you have stopped 'doing' and takes full advantage by using those moments to take a nap and recharge its batteries.

There is another reason why we fall asleep. As we lay there, novices at getting out of our heads, we might come across uncomfortable or even painful thoughts entering our awareness. The mind and body, clever as they are and built to protect us, recognise this and as a way of defending us from further anxiety, make us fall asleep, so that the negative thought can't bother us. The more I learn about the human mind and body, the more I am amazed. We are indeed fascinating creations (which is partly why, at the age of 49, I signed up to do an A Level in Psychology in 2020).

In that room that October in 2014 there were so many wonderful, fascinating humans lying there, each with their own reasons to fall asleep. Each having found the bravery and self-compassion to enrol and turn up, were now lying there, trying as best they could to pay attention to their big toe, while their heads hurled memories and anxieties at them. One recently retired lady had worked as a paediatric nurse in intensive care all her career. Decades spent caring for babies and children ill or in pain, many suffering, many who didn't make it. Another lady in her seventies, had been sent by her daughter, in the hope that it would help her with memory loss and ill health (she has sadly passed away since then). Another, very bright lady, who had lectured in psychology and had decades of experience with meditation and religion, was there to try and find focus as a self-employed academic who worked from home. Another younger lady had two children under five and was trying to find a way to struggle less with her new role as a home-based mother. Similarly, another lady was a mother of teen daughters and now that they were both out of primary school and apparently needed her less, she too was struggling to understand her new role. One gentleman was a sculptor, also working from home, and finding it hard to focus on completing works of art for art's sake, for himself, but only able to concentrate if the work was commissioned by a client with a specific deadline. There were two authors. One like the sculptor was trying to reignite his creativity and focus. The other was struggling with the pain his daughter was feeling post-divorce, pain that had led her to self-harm and depression. And finally there was a beautiful, brave girl who had just started Uni and was helping herself recover from anxiety and bulimia. Mindfulness isn't just for one gender or one age group. It is for anyone seeking to find happiness, one breath at a time.

All these beautiful souls were trying as best as they could to pay attention to their bodies, with the purpose of learning to concentrate on the sensations in the present moment, of getting out of their heads and away from the self-judging habits that caused their stress, anxiety or self-loathing. Trying to just be. But as minds do, are built to do, they think. They bring back hard memories. They propel us into the uncertainty of the future. And to protect ourselves, we switch off. And most of us switched off, waking up to realise that we had missed whole parts of our bodies. That we last remembered paying attention on our knee, but our fabulous teacher was now talking about the shoulders. Where all the parts in between had gone, no one who dropped off knew. And it didn't matter.

Including me. I dropped off quite a few times. Why? What thoughts was my self-defence mechanism protecting me from? Why was I there? I was about to find out.

Somewhere between week two and three something truly amazing happened; I stopped crying. One day I got that sick feeling in my stomach mid-meditation and I noticed it. I caught it. I paused. I breathed into it. I sent my attention to my chest instead and felt my breath. I told myself everything was going to be okay. And the tears didn't come.

For the first time in 120 days I had been able to be sad without my sadness controlling me. To feel pain, but not suffer. Just two weeks in to this new-found skill, I found a way of saving myself from perpetual crying. From constant sadness. I found my Saving Grace.

After that I started to look forward to the mindful mornings. To seeing my fellow life-travellers. Week three we learnt a new way of meditating called a sitting practice; using the breath and the body to 'gather our scattered mind'. As I sat upright and dignified on the chair, with a cushion under my feet due to my below-average height, my mind would often become lost in thought, wandering off to things I could have done in the past to prevent the current situation, then on to things I had to fix around the house, then things I had to sort out for the kids. Constantly working away in the background, looking out for my survival, as it is built to do. Occasionally it would wander forwards into the future, planning what I would do once I was stronger; the looming first Christmas with HIM by HER side, the next lot of students for my tutoring business, and then it would stop. I couldn't think any further than two months ahead. It was just too scary. But luckily each time feelings got overwhelming, our teacher's voice would be there, encouraging me to return intentionally to THIS moment, to THIS breath. To use my breath as an anchor to reconnect to the here and now. And in doing so, the scary feelings settled, softened, lessened. Being on that chair got easier. The small space of the sad voices in my head opened up with each breath and my world got wider; I could see things from a different, less intense perspective. From now. In that broad and present place, I was able to notice my mind's habitual thought patterns. I learnt my limits of what I could and couldn't sit with without wobbling. And I learnt to accept my proneness to wobble without putting myself down or worrying that the wobbling wouldn't stop. This new skill – the sitting practice – had given me a new way to take care of myself that didn't require wine or a 5km run. It gave me freedom.

Before the end of the third session we had also been taught a shorter meditation called the 3-minute breathing space. I still use it daily today when things get a little hectic: traffic delays on the way to one of the many schools I teach in, late invoices, tricky teenagers or their challenges, ex-husbands, a sick mum ...

I like to do it in the car in between locations or when I've arrived somewhere after a dash. We were taught to start by sitting upright and dignified with our eyes closed (I really don't care who walks past my car when I'm sitting) and once we are grounded to:

1. Turn our attention to our thinking mind and notice the thoughts a little bit like events on a screen. What am I thinking? Can I label them like mental events? Then what feelings are those thoughts provoking? Are these unpleasant or uncomfortable? And what body sensations are these emotions provoking? Is anything in my body tight or heavy?

2. Next we were encouraged to turn away from our thoughts to our breath in our chest and our belly, using it to anchor us back to the present moment. What movements were we aware of as we exhaled and inhaled?

3. Finally, we were invited to broaden our attention beyond our breath to our whole body and face, noticing our posture and our facial expressions, becoming aware of tension, contractions and resistance in our lower body.

Those three minutes work wonders; as we go from one doing activity to another, they offer us the opportunity to stop and come back to sensing. To being. The home-practice from that week got easier as did the diarising of what turned up, what was easy, what was challenging. I was beginning to create a habit of 'being with' (the true definition of meditation) that would stay with me and become a way of life. Of LIVING.

Week four of the Mindfulness miracle, as it felt like, started to tackle tricky challenges, as we were taught to recognise difficulty. Well into the short days and long, dark nights of November

2014, darker things were going to come out of the shadows. Looking back on the three painful and useless counselling CBT sessions I had had, I have to stop myself from getting cross, now that I know there are certain, simple questions that you can ask yourself, which help you recognise your negative thought patterns in a moment. Each time I have used them with the many participants on my own MBCT courses, their response is so great, they have such a feeling of enlightenment. (Not every MBSR course or teacher includes them, as technically they help detect a depression relapse, in order to prevent it.)

However, as you read this I wonder how many of these questions you would answer yes to? Most are about how you relate to yourself, such as:

'I'm no good'
'Why can't I ever succeed'
'I've let people down'
'I wish I were a better person'
'I'm so disappointed in me'
'I'm so weak'
'I can't get things together'
'I can't get started'
'What's wrong with me?'
'I hate myself'
'I'm worthless'
'I'm a loser'
'What's the matter with me?'
'I feel so helpless'.
'I can't finish anything'

Others are about the wider world, such as 'I feel like I am up against the world', 'no-one understands me', 'nothing feels good anymore', 'I can't stand this anymore', 'I wish I were somewhere else', 'something has to change', 'my life is a mess', 'it's just not worth it' or 'I wish I could disappear'.

And others are about the future, such as, 'I don't think I can go on', 'my life's not going the way I want it to', 'I'll never make it' or 'my future is bleak'.

The mindful, compassionate use of these questions can help you identify how often these thoughts arise when you are low and, more importantly, how far you believe them. When we are scared, sad or worried, these kinds of thoughts can seem completely convincing, as if they are the actual truth. What the 8-week course taught me and the others that day, was that they are NOT the truth. They are just symptoms of stress or depression, just a fictitious voice. Once we know that, we can step back from these fictional thoughts and make a choice to believe them or not. We can CHOOSE. We have a CHOICE. We have CONTROL. In the best of scenarios we just need to notice them, acknowledge them and LET THEM GO for what they are: THOUGHTS NOT FACTS.

When I am teaching, I regularly check in with my participants and ask them what Mindfulness has come to mean to them. Mostly, as it did for me, they say it means to be in the now, to have skills to stay calm, to be focused on a path to being happy. They rarely say it is a way of blocking out or pushing away bad thoughts. Because from the onset Mindfulness always admits that life includes things which are difficult. Shit happens. But the Mindfulness approach gives you a way to handle that shit, so that the shit doesn't control you. It gives you the ability to become free from the habit of reacting to life from a place of fear. It gives you the skills to respond from a place of self-love. It gives you peace.

That week, half way through the 8-week course, our teacher explained what now seems so obvious: that we react in one of three ways when our survival instinct, our amygdala, is sad, worried or scared:

1. We walk away from this unpleasant moment, into our heads

2. We attach ourselves to this moment, refusing to let go of it, even if it is unhelpful, or recall an experience we aren't having but want

3. We get angry with THIS moment and will it to go away, or avoid future moments we don't want to happen.

None of these reactions are helpful, so we need a way to deal with feelings of aversion or attachment, of anger or avoidance. That is the difficulty that I began to learn to sit with on week four; the ability to sit WITH rather than be averse to, thoughts of another person in HIS life; the ability to let go of wonderful but torturous memories of many, happier times; the ability to keep anger from raging and work towards forgiveness, of him and myself; the ability to face the future, as a single mother of three, with an ended marriage of 21 years to a man I still loved dearly, without being scared. The ability to feel at peace.

That week we also learnt a Mindfulness practice that offers a great way of connecting with the here and now without having to sit still. Yay! I hear all of you, fidgety bottoms yell. Mindful walking felt odd at first, but personally I soon began to find delight in miniscule movements of this amazing thing I had always taken for granted; my body.

In that fairly small room, with white walls, a skylight, and huge orange cushions, the 12 of us were taught the art of mindful walking which goes like this:

- You need a space big enough for about seven to ten paces.
- You stand with feet parallel, with about six inches between them, soft knees, arms hanging by your side, looking softly ahead.
- Drop your attention to the soles of your feet and notice the sensation of the weight of your body as it makes contact with the floor (a few tiny knee bends or flexes can make this sensation more noticeable).
- Then start walking by shifting your weight into the right leg, noticing how sensations change in the left leg, as the right leg now supports your weight.
- Lift the left heel slowly and as you do notice muscles around the left calf, as you raise the foot off the ground leaving just the toes touching the floor, then lift it completely, move it forward through the air and gently place it back on the floor starting with the heel. As your left foot makes total contact with the floor, shift your body weight from the right to the left, noticing the new sensations in that left supporting leg, and noticing the sensations in the now loose right leg.
- Now lift the right foot as you did the left, move it forward, place it down again and send your attention

to the right heel, and flatten the foot to the ground, shifting the weight back onto the right, becoming aware of changing sensations in the right and left feet and legs.

We moved like this slowly around the room, making sure that we didn't crash (or laugh) and soon all we were aware of were our sensations, our movements, our MOMENTS. In THAT moment. The simple technique anchored us, as our breath had in the body scan, and in the sitting practice and in the three-minute breathing space. By the end of the few minutes of mindful walking, we were totally appreciating the wonder of walking. Throughout we were encouraged to notice our wandering minds and to use the real, present moment, physical experience to gently, kindly, non-judgementally bring us back.

This skill was so simple, but effective. I remember adapting it at high speed to noticing my legs on an endorphin-inducing treadmill run. But nowadays I have slowed back down to enjoying mindful walking in the cemetery opposite the primary school, or around the grounds of a beautiful school I teach at in Kingston at lunchtime, or when walking the dog on the common. Each step is an anchor to this moment. Stepping one foot at a time to get nowhere other than right here, right now.

Four weeks into the course I had four new skills but more importantly, I had my life back. I entered the room on week five feeling stronger than I had in nearly a whole year, and ready for any suggestion our teacher might make – which in week five was to turn towards the difficult. There is a clear method to the 8-week course which was becoming evident. For the first two sessions you learn to reconnect with your breath and even more your body, to listen to it, to allow it to whisper (or shout) to you all the messages you haven't been listening to while you have been busy doing, stressing, fearing, hurting. Then in the next two weeks you learn to notice where and what your thoughts are, and to use your breath as an anchor to come back to the present moment. Now was the time to start to deal with some of those difficult thoughts that prevent us from being the happy, joyous and peaceful person we were when we came into this world.

There will always be pain ... a sentence I say now and again (such as after visiting my mum, who suffers from dementia and chronic spinal arthritis) and have shared with many of my students of varying ages. But if you adopt an attitude of kindness to yourself, you develop the ability to stare at this pain that keeps drawing your attention away time and time again, and to notice the predominant body sensations that arise in the moment you do, with friendly, gentle awareness. You even become able to notice the pulling of the thoughts without dread, to feel those tugs and just stay where you are, watching thoughts unravel, without getting caught in them, simply by paying attention to what is arising in your body at the same time. In other words, you begin to relate differently to the painful thoughts. And by doing so you can turn these thoughts from persistent pain, which will turn to suffering, to discomfort and eventually to pass. By paying attention to the body sensations they cause, you can now respond to painful thoughts as they arise, not just react to their pain. You can choose.

And that is what I began to learn on that wintery Thursday morning in SW4; the hitherto nonsensical idea that if you allow yourself to notice and feel the pain, to allow the pain to exist, it will go. Now it makes so much obvious sense. Unless someone is actually stabbing you with a sharp object, the pain has to come from somewhere else. Which means it has to come from a thought. And as thoughts aren't facts, they are simply where we are choosing to place our attention in any given moment, then we can choose to lay our attention somewhere less painful. Like our breath. Hey presto, the pain goes away, even if just momentarily. Magic. Well Mindfulness actually, but yes pretty much magic.

In case I wasn't clear enough: turn to the irritation, the tension, the fear, the pain, allow yourself to feel it in your body … and watch it gradually get softer until it isn't there anymore.

While I DO want the simplicity of it to be made clear, I don't want to make you think it is always easy to achieve. One of the many wonderful attitudes encouraged by Mindfulness is to suspend expectation. So, while in one practice you might be able to watch painful thoughts, feel their sensations and stay in the moment, rather than start contracting or crying, the next time you practice, the opposite might happen. The key is to help yourself relax into the experience by setting the intention to not try to make things different as they arise. To let go. To let be. To allow.

I am drawn to a memory of my years at Arthur Andersen, where everything we did revolved around looking at situations, finding places where things weren't working as well as they could, and come up with ways to make them better, to change them, in the name of profit. At the core of this 'organisational improvement' is the concept of not accepting what is going on, of trying to create other states of being. It is what the human brain is built to do – look out for things that threaten our survival and strive to change them. Now that I have trained extensively with the Oxford Mindfulness Centre in how to bring Mindfulness to the workplace, I see a different, more compassionate way of 'doing' organisational development, or of 'doing' continuous improvement. I'll leave that for my next book (but in the meantime you can check my website for some ideas.)

I am also drawn to remembering the father figure in the fabulous kids' movie The Croods (if you haven't seen it, tonight is the night). This prehistoric man lives in constant fear and creates a world for himself and his family that blocks out what is actually happening. And it takes his daughter's younger, relaxed, curious pair of eyes to dare to see the magic of the sunrise. To 'be alive and know it', as Jon Kabat-Zinn says.

Mindfulness can't turn back the clock and make us younger, but it can give us back the youthful carefree state we had before life happened to us. Before fear and hurt crept in.

Mindfulness practices can strip the power away from those painful thoughts and give US the power back, the freedom from brooding or rumination. At least that is what it gave me that week and I have seen it in most of my 6000 students since then. By sitting up tall, strong and dignified, and opening up to what we are experiencing, we gain clarity; the clarity that distinguishes fictional thoughts from factual moment by moment experience. And with that clarity comes the strength to stop supressing or avoiding. To notice, to allow, and to choose not to get pulled away from this moment, from this beautiful breath. And the key to that ability to allow is compassion; kindness to ourselves for what we are experiencing. Caring so much that we sit, feel, breathe. Opening the door to let happiness, joy and peace back in.

How can I show myself compassion you ask? What does that look like, self-compassion? Remembering the kind listening of the Reverend, who assured me my kids would be okay despite the turmoil I was in, despite seeing me cry, Mindfulness encourages us to use the same approach with ourselves. When mid-practice feelings or sensations became overwhelming, we are guided to simply say "I'm okay. I feel sad and that's OK. I can allow myself to be open to it. It's OK". And to stay there. To stick with the sensations, breathe with them, repeating those words and with each exhalation opening, softening. This doesn't mean that you are giving up to the sadness or fear, or becoming resigned to it, letting go of control or power, waiting for it to move on. No, allowing is watching the sensation with kindness, telling yourself with compassionate conviction that it's ok to feel this way, just being. Not being sad, scared or resigned. Just being. Breathing in. Breathing out.

So by the end of just five weeks, ten hours with my wonderful teacher and fellow healing-journey-travellers, and after many more hours in between practicing alone on my bed, in the car, on a bench on Wandsworth Common, I had learnt how to listen to my body, notice where my thoughts were, realise they were just that, thoughts, acknowledge the pain of my separation, watch it, come back to this beautiful moment and move on. Something I had been trying to do for years, became a reality in weeks.

Week six helped me make sense of what I had been experiencing for a fortnight with some more scientific, meaty learning to add to the Mindfulness bone. We had already started to consider thoughts as transient mental events rather than facts. So negative thoughts, leading to negative moods, can also be seen as transient states of mind. This is totally freeing, when you have been experiencing depression for four months (that you are aware of, and probably longer) and have begun to see it softening. I suddenly began to truly believe the Mindfulness 'hype' and to realise that I had power over my thoughts, not them over me and my feelings. I had the power to let them go. Just by bringing my attention to my breath. By coming closer to each breath, I was able to get some distance between me and my negative, soul-destroying thoughts, to see them from a different, less attached perspective.

And then something else wonderful happened; I began to understand why my marriage hadn't made it further than the twenty-one years it did (not to be sniffed at). Rather than be a prisoner to the old thought patterns that made me angry with HIM or sad about my situation, I was able to understand things with compassion. It dawned on me that we all handle situations with the skills we have at the time. My past baggage and fear of being abandoned, had led me to react to his distance with anxiety, anger and bitterness. In return, his past baggage and fear that sticking around would lead to further arguing (as it had done in his parents' marriage), had led him to react to my bitterness with avoidance by choosing not to leave Portugal with us. Neither of us had meant to hurt the other. We were, sadly, depressed and reacting from fear. One reacting with anxiety and the other with avoidance. We had no ability at that time to respond with love, a love that had been alive for 18 years. Despite the three clear bits of evidence before us, aged 3, 6 and 8, the tyrannical negative thoughts made it impossible for our actions to come from a place of love. So they came from fear. They came and they conquered.

And let me clarify that none of that was fed to me by some sort of psychoanalysis in our group sessions. Mindfulness isn't psychotherapy. That awareness arose in me. From me. And some of it might even be wrong, but it all revolved around having an openness about what was and was not fact. And creating space for compassion and self-compassion to forgive others and myself.

So, in SW4, with the help of my teacher-come-friend and my forever friend, my breath, I was able to realize that my thoughts about my ended marriage were not facts, and by doing that I was able to know that there had been love and that there was still love, just in a different way. That I was still loving and loveable. It was a great Christmas present. Who needed profiteroles?

By learning to look at my thoughts, which were clearly indicating beliefs held deep in my subconscious mind since my father had died when I was two, I gained the freedom from the spiralling low moods I had suffered for four months, which had come from my habitual, automatic, negative thoughts patterns: I am not worthy or loveable. I had become free from the unanswered question, previously repeated time and time again in my mind: Why? Why me? Why didn't he stay? I now had the skills to stop ruminating over that question and to take actions that would help me get out of the low mood. I had my breath back. I was no longer in a place where I wanted to just GIVE UP. I had my breath, the knowledge that thoughts aren't facts and I was determined to use both to change the way I had been feeling. For my kids. For me. Forever.

As an MBCT teacher I now have this from our teacher training book to use with my students ... and myself:

From thoughts come actions. From actions come all sorts of consequences. In which thoughts will we invest? Our great task is to see them clearly, so that we can choose which ones to act on and which simply to let be.
—JOSEPH GOLDSTEIN '89

MBCT isn't a theory. It is a practice. It is practical. I have had many, often heated, debates, where I explain that there is little point in teaching people about the brain and how it works, unless you also teach people practically how to work WITH their brain. So let me share with you, as our teacher did on week six (and my wonderful teacher trainer Dr Patrizia Collard after her), some ideas for how you can have a different perspective about your thoughts:

- Imagine you are sat somewhere and watch your thoughts come in as a cloud, or a bus, or a leaf on a stream, or credits on a screen, or sushi on a travellator, or on a balloon in your hand, or as music on a score ... then stay sat where you are, on a bench, or bus stop, or by the riverbank, or at the cinema, or on the barstool, or holding the balloon, or reading the music sheet, and let go, watch the thought move away, leave without feeling you have to follow it.

- Think of your thoughts as arising from urges, that have arisen from body sensations, that have arisen from feelings ... and see if you can notice that feeling, emotion or mood, that caused this thought, all as just links in a chain of thought events. Chains that can be broken by you just noticing. As Jon Kabat-Zinn says in his definition of Mindfulness: it is the awareness that arises from paying attention. What awareness arises for you?

- See your thought as a mental event: Where are you? When is it (past or future)? Who is there? What can you see? Hear? How are people acting? But avoid asking why, avoid getting involved in the thought. Just watch it. And remember it isn't true. You don't need to deal with the event. Just watch it and then watch it disappear.

- When you notice your thoughts, write them down (doing this first thing about dreams is useful too). On paper you can observe them with less emotion than in your head and so they are less overwhelming, less likely to make you react. More likely to enable you to respond. Words in ink on paper have less power than as dialogue in your head. As I am always telling my students, thoughts in the small space of your head appear bigger than when you let them out verbally or in writing into the big, wide, world outside your head.

- For some thoughts which might be particularly difficult, as the ones we were encouraged to face that week, it's better to set some time aside and invite them in intentionally as part of a practice or sit. This can be more helpful. Perhaps do a 3-minute breathing space practice first to start with a grounded, balanced mind. This will give you the wisdom to see thoughts for what they are, even difficult ones. Then you can label the feelings and emotions as you notice them arising from the thoughts. And then, however crazy it sounds, you can try to have a compassionate curiosity about the feeling. "Oh how curious that that has turned up', you can say to yourself softly, gently, kindly.

Assuming you aren't crumbled on the floor in a heap of uncontrollable laughter at the prospect of 1. Inviting hard thoughts in on purpose and 2. Talking to them with curiosity rather than anger, sadness, fear or frustration, here are some other tips (and if you are on the floor, enjoy the laughter, it's good for you, then get up and read on!).

No-one wants to be unhappy. Sometimes when you are depressed it feels like a safe place to be as you know it and are scared of the unknown, including happiness. Your ego encourages you to stay depressed, self-pitiful, feeling pain. Because feeling pain is better than feeling the numb nothingness, which is the alternative. But no one truly wants to be unhappy. Everyone deserves and in fact has a duty to be happy, since our mood affects those around us. So, it is important to learn some wisdom about how to deal with unhappiness, for our sake and for those in our lives, which is pretty much anyone you come across when you leave your front door, pick up the phone, or write an email. So here goes, how can you tell a low mood is on its way? How can you be a low mood detective?

1. Become familiar with what your difficulty is triggered by; is it something that happens to you, a memory from the past or a worry about the future? Even if it was something tiny, make a note of it.

2. Become familiar with what thoughts your low mood leads to. Are they about you, the world or the future?

3. Notice the sensations in your body; do your hands and

feet twitch, does your heart beat faster, does your breath change, does your head feel dizzy? Do you get hot? What tightens?

4. Notice what the urges are that you get. Do you get into freeze, flee or flight mode?

5. Are you able to detect habits or patterns of thoughts and actions, which go on to increase or keep you in this low mood? Are you going over the same thing time and time again, or pushing difficulty away? Are you fighting with your thoughts, refusing to accept how you feel?

It isn't easy but it is simple: when this occurs be firm with yourself about saying to yourself that thoughts aren't facts; be patient, knowing that everything passes in its own time, not always when we want it to; most importantly be kind to yourself, remembering to be curious about thoughts and feelings, not judgemental. Love you. Love this breath. Breathe.

Before sending us on our way that lunchtime just before 1pm, two weeks before the end of the eight-week course, we did a meditation I love and that is loved my most of my students. I believe it originates from Jon Kabat-Zinn's book 'wherever you go, there you are' and is beautifully simple yet wonderfully powerful. The Mountain Meditation invites you to use imagery to remember the true meaning of being in and able to live, this moment, of sensing this moment, from a steady place, from a strong place. Start by sitting on a chair or cross legged on a cushion or the floor, with your hands palm down on your knees and imagining a mountain; the most beautiful one you have seen or been to (I like to think of Lanin in Argentina, a majestic, extinct volcano he and I climbed when I was 6 weeks pregnant with No.1).

Pay attention to how tall the mountain, how wide, whether the peak is snowy, how steep its slopes are and how firm and steady its base is. Then turn your attention to your body and incorporate the mountain into it, imagining your head as the peak, your arms as the slopes and your lower back and seat as the base. Allow yourself to imagine that you are the mountain; a still, centred, rooted, present, breathing mountain. And just like mountains stay unshaken in stormy weather, so too can you stay grounded and calm with any stormy thoughts that appear and bash your flanks, stay rooted where you are as the thoughts move on. By the end of week six I was a mountain of strength. Maybe just a Scafell Pike or a Ben Nevis, rather than Everest, but mountainous in my new-found steadiness. After that, I used my Mindfulness to climb Africa's second highest peak in Morocco (see chapter 10 below), and more recently I used it to climb Mount Kilimanjaro in 2020 for Alzheimer's Society.

What could Mindfulness do for you in just six weeks?

The last two weeks of the course have a slightly different focus. We start to look ahead. Week seven started by helping us learn how to take care of ourselves. If we don't know the things we truly enjoy and we forget to build them into our daily lives, and risk spiralling towards exhaustion. A lack of daily, nourishing activities leads to an imbalance in our lives, where only work and stress exist, which is totally depleting for the soul and body. Unfortunately, it can be with the best intention that some people work 'too' hard, in their attempt to be conscientious or make a difference to their families or the world. Or they need to feel they are doing well at work to feel good about themselves, to feel confident. But ironically the truth is that this is counter-productive and dangerous to our mental and physical wellbeing. As we neglect what nourishes us, we risk entering a spiral of problems. Perhaps we start to suffer from disturbed or lack of sleep (finding it hard to get to sleep, or waking up in the middle of the night). This can lead to feeling less energetic or even have aches and pains in your body. This physical low place can trigger mental ill health, such as feelings of shame or guilt, a lack of joy. Which can lead to depression. That place on the floor where you are physically and mentally exhausted.

So to prevent this we need to realise that our general wellbeing is affected by what we do hourly, daily, weekly, monthly and from one year to the next. It can be really helpful to stop, as we did in week seven, and analyse how you spend your time. That week, we listed, silently, in reflection, all the things we did in a week on a piece of A4 paper. Then we reviewed that list and labelled each activity as either nourishing, that is, adding a feeling of being alive, or draining or depleting, namely taking away from my sense of being alive. Obviously the mood we are in might affect how we view certain activities. For example, if we are tired or low, tidying, cleaning, paying bills or dealing with some emails, might feel depleting. However, if we take a different perspective, from a good place, we might see these activities as adding value to our lives. And knowing that, can give be enough to seek being grounded, so that we can undertake the supposedly depleting activities more skilfully, in the knowledge that some activities may never feel like a barrel of laughs but don't need to be painful either. So we looked at trying to do more of what nourished us, and have a different mindset when it came to the things that had hitherto felt depleting. Mindful time management. Good stuff.

One great example of a nourishing activity is exercise. Even if you don't consider yourself to be fit or sporty, as many of my students claim, you can take a ten-minute walk, or a stretching class online, or yoga or tai-chi, or go for a swim, or go horse riding. And yes, if you feel up to it a jog around the common. Don't think about day two, three or four. One day at a time, until you have found a routine in a gentle, self-compassionate, non-judgmental way. Not caring what you look like in leggings next to the marathon runners who pass you. And if you miss a day because you just can't be bothered, that's ok too! Once exercise is in your daily routine, it is there for you to build mental strength proactively ahead of difficulty, when and if it happens.

Another way in which analysing our activities can help, is as a remedy for times when we feel low. Identifying what feeds our soul and making a promise to do more of it is a start. But what can also be useful is to understand why it makes us feel happy, joyous, alive, so that we can choose it as a strategy of getting out of a low mood (and we know that Mindfulness works as well as if not better than medication). It can be as simple as writing a post-it note that says something like "if you read this and feel rubbish, do yourself a favour, find your list of fave activities and move".

Looking again at our list of nourishing activities, we determined whether they gave us a sense of pleasure or mastery. Pleasure comes when we do something just because we can, without shame or guilt or justification, such as; a bath (with candles and essential oils if that's your 'thang'), a nap (with your favourite pillow and throw), making or eating your favourite food (preferably low sugar or caffeine free, to prevent too much short lived stimulation followed by a rapid low), a facemask, doing your nails, watching the footie or your favourite TV programme (be careful not to binge watch, as that nurtures impatience), or getting your hair cut, your nails done or a shave at the barbers. Perhaps you like talking to people on the phone or going for a walk with a friend and their dog, or you have a hobby such as acting, singing, playing an instrument, gardening, painting, pottery, crochet, knitting or DIY. Maybe you like to shop or listen to music. Or go to a play or an exhibition. Whatever floats your boat. But start by listing what you do that you enjoy, simply for the enjoyment of it, with presence. And you will perhaps realise it has been a while since you did it. You might make a point of doing it as soon as you put the pen down. But you will also have it there in your mind as a way out of a low mood. As a choice to get up and get happy.

Another alternative we explored about how to take care of yourself when you find yourself in a low mood, is to do something that will give you a sense of satisfaction, mastery, achievement or control. Like sorting out a drawer or cupboard that is full of unwanted objects, or spring cleaning one room (don't aim for the whole house as that will be overwhelming). Perhaps you have friends or family who live abroad who you could write a letter or email to? Or sit down for a few hours and clear some emails you have been avoiding? These are all activities that will make you feel good about yourself. Feel proud and positive. Needed and worthwhile. Things that will lift you and your mood up. And don't forget to congratulate yourself afterwards, even half way through – self-motivation is a skill, so praise yourself when you do it.

So in week seven of this 8-week path to peace, we learnt how to make the conscious decision to reduce depleting actions and increase the time dedicated to nourishing ourselves, all with the aim of being able to regulate our mood, whether we are in a happy place or to prevent a relapse of depression. Our daily experiences can become strategic tools for coping with low mood. If we develop these habits before low mood sets in, we are more able to stick with them when strong negative thoughts turn up, rather than just say 'why bother' to ourselves and give up. They keep us off the kitchen floor. So grab a pen and paper and see what is revealed to you.

However, sometimes even with a list of good stuff, if you are ungrounded, it isn't a given that you will know what would you serve me in that particular moment of difficulty. The lightbulb idea of what we need that instant might not pop up automatically, so first of all we are instructed to ground ourselves, to allow space and openness to focus away from low mood and on a positive activity, by doing a three-minute breathing space with an additional step. After expanding our awareness to our body from our breath, having found a sensation that was less than comfortable, we were encouraged to breathe into it and out from it too, without too much expectation, but rather with a curiosity as to whether we would soften a little or open up. And in that soft, open, accepting space, we would be able to choose the next step. To choose to take care of ourselves. To choose to be happy.

In that soft, grounded place we can know what our soul needs. We can ask gently 'What do I need for ME right here, right now? How can I best take care of myself?'

And whatever pops up, we are encouraged to try and do it with curiosity, like an experiment. Suspending expectation about feeling great fast. Just being open to the experience, without judging it second by second, waiting for a change in mood. And play around with the many options we had previously listed.

Or add to that list. Even if you have a favourite go-to activity, like a swim, the idea is to try to break the monotony and automatic response, by experimenting with a new pool, or trying a variety of activities, not just the same one. Often just the fact that you are doing something new can trigger a sense of freshness and joy; by exploring a new park or trying a new food, you can spark new neurons and counteract the desire to withdraw, which often comes with difficulty. I have since expanded my list to include so many things I wouldn't have before – walking the circumference of Richmond park instead of doing a 10km on the treadmill. Baking with spelt rather than avoiding baked goods altogether. Going for a swim in the Cornish North Coast or North Sea! And it has been fun!

And finally, although I wholly believe in miracles, try not to expect them. Do your best. But remember the seven pillars of Mindfulness as you try to take care of yourself; don't judge how well you are doing this self-care activity; don't strive to do it better or longer than necessary; be patient as the low mood decreases; have a beginner's mind even if you have had a candlelit bath before; accept whatever feelings come to your attention; trust that they will pass; and let go of any past 'failures' to improve your mood. You are making a self-compassionate attempt to love yourself in this moment. In this breath. Right now. That's all that matters. If your mood changes dramatically super-fast, great. If it just improves a little and takes time to do so, that's great too. No pressure.

I hope this doesn't sound patronising or over-simplistic, but it really is that easy to get back control of your mood shifts. I've been there, experienced low moods jumping out at me out of the blue, when things seemed to be going so well just the day before. I have woken up feeling exhausted for no apparent reason. Apathetic, despite going to bed full of beans and positive. How did I get out of that place? I learnt to tell myself "OK Anna, you are feeling a little stressed. Don't panic. It will pass. You won't be stressed for long. Breathe". And the more you practice that, the shorter the periods of low mood become, until they are nearly not there at all.

By making a commitment to take care of myself and taking the steps to know how to do it, those times when I over-generalised, or assumed things would not get better or would even get worse, when I felt like I was back to square one, stopped controlling me. By pausing, taking care of myself and noticing the moment, just that one moment, I was able after seven weeks to make sense of what had happened. And to realise I was ok. I had developed the ability to see and feel the tug of old behaviours or negative ways of thinking and not be dragged down by them. I was able to stay strong. I learnt, each time low mood appeared, to tell myself, 'Anna, you are not weak, you are not useless. It isn't your fault.' Having been given permission by the Reverend to love myself, I had spent seven weeks learning how.

And that seventh week closed with another amazing meditation

– the LOVING KINDNESS MEDITATION. Until you have tried it, you can't fathom the power of these words and imagery. Of love. You sit. Connect. Breathe. Ground. Then bring an image to mind of yourself and send good wishes, warmth and kindness, to yourself by saying "May I be safe, may I be happy, may I be free from suffering, may I be at ease". Then pause and really feel the self-love. Allow your own image to go into the background and now bring to mind someone you love (a friend or rellie) and send them heart felt thoughts of compassion, of kindness and say the phrase again "May you be safe, may you be happy, may you be free from suffering, may you be at ease". And take time to send off these thoughts to them. The third step of the Loving Kindness practice is to bring to mind someone fairly neutral (a neighbour or someone you see daily, maybe a bus driver or shop assistant) and invite loving feelings in for them also, repeating the phrase "May you be safe, may you be happy, may you be free from suffering, may you be at ease". Next, allow yourself to bring to mind someone tricky (not the most difficult person in your life) and repeat for them too "May you be safe, may you be happy, may you be free from suffering, may you be at ease". Now let all four sit in your awareness and notice how it feels to send them loving kindness, saying to them "May you be safe, may you be happy, may you be free from suffering, may you be at ease". Finally watch those four fade into the background and let your feelings of love spread to your whole neighbourhood, the city you are in as far as your mind will stretch, and send out feelings of love to everyone on this planet who might be suffering through anxiety, war or sickness. Once you have allowed your heart to extend these wishes to all seven billion souls on earth, allow them to fade and come back to the body and the breath and steady yourself, noticing the warmth and love deep in your heart and now also in every fibre of your body and your being.

My pen is down taking in the love. It feels odd to continue writing after such a beautiful and profound practice.

The eighth and final week of my 'fantastic voyage' brought me full circle to the body scan. To noticing with self-compassion how differently I related to it, compared to week one. No longer a trial, a test to stay awake, to stop ruminating, I (and I think we) welcomed it, melted into it, relished every moment of the 40 minutes 'massage'. By befriending the body scan we had befriended our minds, our bodies, ourselves.

But there was still a little work to do. To ensure the knowledge and skills would live on way beyond the eight weeks, we had to make a plan to safeguard this new mindful way of living. We set our intentions about how to maintain the new habits and even extend them to new, deeper knowledge. When encouraged to identify why I wanted to keep up my practice, why I wanted to carry on taking care of myself, I had a newfound reassurance; I deserved it. I had learnt to love myself. I had learnt to live in THIS breath, THIS moment, and it had given me the conviction that I WAS WORTH IT. I was lighter, brighter, and determined to lead the life I had always desired. I was softer, kinder, to myself and others, and I was smiling. It would still be a while until I got to where I am today, but I knew that by sitting with my thoughts, the light had got in through the cracks that had once seemed scary. And I was (gently) fired to explore how I could turn that light, those embers, in to a fire, with a light so strong that it would shine not just in me, but in others too. I truly felt like a phoenix rising from the flames of her own despair, towards skies of love and light, of faith and possibility. And much needed fun!

I have shared my journey on the 8 week MBSR course, so that you can have a better understanding of what it entails, as one option to help you reduce stress and low mood in your life. Obviously, there are many ways to learn Mindfulness and meditation, such as by reading books or listening to meditation audios on an App. But I can't emphasise enough the power of attending the 8 week course; of sharing a common goal with the group, being held by the group, sparking your inner compassion by accompanying others on their journey, and having someone other than yourself to be accountable to, so that you turn up week after week, in the name of self-love, presence and peace. It takes the human brain at least 6 weeks to rewire pathways, and if you are enrolled in an 8 week course you stand a better chance of staying committed and showing up until the end. So yes, to reduce your daily stress, do follow the meditations I have scripted here, or email me for an audio, but if you are in a place of low mood, reach out to a professional rather than try to DIY right now. Whichever path is right for you, start now; learn to live in this moment – it's a good one.

Part three: LEARN TO LEAD THE LIFE YOU DESIRE

So, having learnt to love myself, rather than blame myself, and having learnt to be in this precious moment, rather than torturing myself with memories of my past, I set about exploring life. Living life. Being alive and knowing it, as the great man says. Re-discovering what I really wanted, enjoyed, desired. Exploring the old, true me inside. And ending up finding something even better.

Without any clear plan I started to explore some of the many bits of advice that popped up once I had started looking; from mediums to self-inquiry experts, from inspirational speakers to intuitive life coaches. I found a new love of yoga and went further to experiment with different types of liberating exercise. And I went away; to creative writing workshops, to stimulating cities, to the tops of mountains, to the sea and to silence. I had no goal in mind. I just felt free to follow my heart's desires, with a twinkle in my eye, a spring in my step and a smile on my face. I left my guilty conscience at home and set off on a journey to entitlement. After over a decade of looking after others' happiness, I put my right to be happy first (well mostly, I am a single mother of three after all).

Thanks to my journey into self-love and present-moment awareness, I was strong in my conviction that I deserved to be happy. I was determined to lead the life I desired.

This is how I did it. The following steps filled me with a sense of loving life. I am sharing them with you in a hope that, if you are feeling a little out of love with life right now, they might inspire you to have some fun. To feel joy. To live the life you desire.

Step 7: Get Listening: invite your spirit guides in

How did I start? Just like I had done the summer before, on a mountain top beneath the stars, once again in 2015 I turned to the Universe's guides. Having been raised by a mother who was always talking about spirits and ghosts, as she called them, I was completely comfortable with seeking insights and advice from another plane. I had also spent many a night as a child talking to my ceiling, asking it questions, knowing someone was listening. In fact, the summer after my adorable grandmother Violeta passed away in 1986, I had been lying in the lower caravan bunkbed about to go to sleep one night (the caravan we had holidayed in with her for many a summer), when I heard the door open and felt someone come in. I told my brother to stop getting up and go to sleep, to which he replied that he was in bed. I fell silent, wary, aware. Aware that someone was in the caravan with us. Then I felt the presence of something just above my open eyes. As if I could feel the heat from a hand hovering above them. I saw nothing. Heard nothing else. But I knew someone was there and I knew it was her. And I was glad she had visited.

So not only was I comfortable with spirits, but I also suspected I could connect with them.

Anyway, having decided to explore the world of psychics, it wasn't hard to find the perfect medium (when you ask, I have learnt, the Universe answers). I asked around, made a few calls, and very soon found the one I got a good vibe from, who would go on to be my teacher and friend to this day.

Mediums aren't gypsies with crystal balls. They aren't loons who wave their hands in the air, making odd noises. They are intuitive, open, connected people, like you and me, who have the ability to communicate with the spirits of those who have died. Human beings have been fascinated with contacting the deceased for 30,000 years. Interest has grown over the last 200 years, not always for the right purpose, as often it is used as a form of entertainment, rather than enlightenment. If you are the kind of person who needs to see things to believe them, you might put psychics down as tricksters or frauds. But I challenge you to meet mine, and see if you don't change your mind. Most of the messages that the mediums I have visited have heard and passed on to me, with details about my life that they simply could not know, have been precise, accurate ... and helpful. But if you don't want the unconditional advice of others, that's your prerogative.

If you are curious however, my experience has been a very positive one over the last seven years since I started going annually at least. Psychic mediums won't tell you what to do, they won't make decisions for you. But they can give you messages from people in your life who have died, that lift you up and reassure you. At times I have felt totally alone. Not lonely, just alone. My father died when I was two. My mother has been poorly for 15 years and too distracted by her own pains to have the ability to take mine on board. My husband became my ex (and even when we were together, we weren't great talkers, rather great doers). My only brother has lived on the other side of the world for the last 20 years. My entire family live a thousand miles away. And although I am blessed with several really, REALLY, good friends (who shouldn't have to hear my woes more than they already have), I am pretty much alone. And sometimes that got to me. So having an opportunity to know that I wasn't actually alone in dealing with my challenges was a godsend. Or a universe-send. Knowing that somewhere in the spirit world I had a network of supporters looking out for me, was exactly the reassurance I needed to accompany me on my new path. No-one has to feel alone.

So February 2015 I drove to my psychic medium in Barnes, South West London. I sat in her gorgeous garden room, and felt instantly relaxed in the warm, scented, welcoming space. She explained that she would invite spirit guides in but couldn't determine who would show up. She also explained that she only invited and communicated with spirit guides of a friendly nature. As it was my first sitting I was a little nervous and had no specific questions about what guidance I was hoping to get, and although I hoped my father would show up, I didn't voice that.

So I sat. She closed her eyes to connect with my energy. Took deep breaths. And within seconds started to describe a person. Me. Hearing someone I had known for two minutes describe me, was a bit like reading my horoscope, but more accurate. She talked without interruption. "You set yourself deadlines, challenges, you are your own worst critic, push yourself, always wanting to do more, go deeper". Sounded familiar. "You are a communicator, that's your forte. You have a lot of gifts, and have had many opportunities to do lots of other jobs before this one". Well I guess so; my twenty-year career had spanned three industries, working in human resources, in hotels, consulting, banking and retail, in the UK and abroad, as well as interior design, and most recently in education. "You have a presence, a confidence, which makes people feel safe, and you are very good at bringing out the best in others and bringing out their potential". My mind went to my second role as trainer, enabling and motivating people to be the best they could, and loving every minute of it. Remembering what it felt like to do a job I loved. I felt better already. She went deeper. Started to share things I had learnt but perhaps ignored. "You have learnt a lesson in your career. You worked as an assistant to a strong man and you thought you were never good enough but it taught you that your boss was no better than you, and that you can be as good as anyone else, as long as you are confident". I knew exactly who she meant and felt slightly stiff as I recalled my year in the corner office in Temple, watching in slight fear as my work was combed for mistakes. Chastised one minute and praised the next by a boss who was simultaneously big hearted and ruthless.

Then her voice softened. "You are a healer now and have been in other lives and you lived in some part of America in very tall woods. You were well thought of and important and had a sense of being responsible for everyone in your community. You still have a huge sense of responsibility to your community, to mankind, you are very concerned about others, more than most." Flashes of memories entered my mind, of feeling responsible for my mother, taking her on holiday with me from the age of sixteen because she had no one else. Dropping everything to help my brother when he got into a pickle. It never felt like a responsibility. Just part of the role of daughter and big sister. "It's a wonderful gift. Spirits like us to use our gifts. Sometimes jobs close and relationships end if you are not using those gifts." Here my eyebrows raised and I nodded. I had been miserable in my first ever job stuck behind a desk in a windowless reservations office, never seeing clients, only hearing them. I had walked away from that as it felt heavy. But I had felt a failure. And again five years later when I had loathed my office in Argentina and taken early maternity leave to get away from what felt so wrong, but again feeling like I had failed. It was reassuring now to know that those jobs weren't for me and that I was actually doing myself a favour because I wasn't using my gifts there.

As for relationships ending for our own good ... that was harder to stomach. But true. I had been hurt early on at twenty when a three year relationship had come to an abrupt end, devastating me, but knew too that it no longer met my heart's desires. I have always wanted to travel. Have always wanted to grab life by the balls, with energy and joy, and that first relationship was with someone who was turning into the opposite of that. So however painful, if a job or a person in your life is quashing the true you, it does start to feel heavy and will eventually end, so you can be the real, authentic you. Hard but liberating. And I knew in my heart that although I still loved my ex-husband, things had been feeling heavy before our split. My energy for travel and new projects wasn't reflected in his desires. My wish for an intense family life, wasn't happy with his job taking him away Monday to Friday. And I knew that in my heart even though it still hurt like hell sometimes.

"There is a new phase coming. You have just finished a 7-year cycle and might be in a rut before the next one comes". I sat up. Cool. This was what I needed to hear. That the shit was going to end. "More responsibility is on its way, in a good way". Fuck, I thought, MORE? Wasn't being a single mother of three with a poorly mum enough? Okay, well bring it on, I thought, whatever. "You can't work somewhere where you have to abide by other people's rules." True, hence why I had loved roaming the Andersen offices in ten different countries, my own boss, as I gathered best practice. And why I had been happy to extend a six-month contract to a year, working for two directors who had trusted my self-motivation and given me lots of room to manoeuvre independently. But ultimately I had broken away back in 2003 and started my own business. Finding that freedom to work by my rules, even if it came with shit loads of responsibility and uncertainty.

"Something else is coming new to do with teaching but as a business". I had quit primary school teaching 6 months earlier due to my depression and was working as a private tutor, teaching up to 14 students a week. But having seen the magic of the MBSR on my life, I was toying with the idea of training to teach Mindfulness to children. Seven years later I have trained three times, to teach primary, secondary and adults, and have taught over 6000 people. But at that time I had no idea what lay ahead. But it felt great to get some reassurance that something good was just around the corner.

"However you are so busy making sure everyone else is okay that you forget to look after your needs," she went on. "Make sure you don't always say yes to everybody. You have a lot of friends who call upon your service and you are always there to help and you don't know how to say no. Give yourself permission to say no, not now." This was true. I recalled a couple of good friends who sometimes got overwhelmed and called on me to help sort out their clutter or just to listen as they ranted on about their woes, disregarding that I was often 'short of time' to deal with my own busy life, never asking others for help. Always 'losing' bits of my 'free' time to get ahead, to help them instead.

"Do you have 3 kids?" she then asked out of nowhere. I did. "They are all very bright. And lively. And different." She went on to describe my son perfectly, giving me tips on how to deal with his mind and imploring me to find a school that would appreciate him. Explaining how he used music to help him sleep, sending shivers down my spine as I write, as while later I discovered he uses music, such as sounds from the Shire, to destress.

"You have a little girl who is a performer, who wears funny clothes," she moved on to my youngest. Again describing her perfectly and confirming what I already suspected, and some had also commented on, that she is very intuitive even at the age of 8. Children in general are intuitive (we are all born with intuition) and we, parents, school, society, push it out of them, constantly asking them to justify their desires, when actually what they are doing is just following their gut, and all we can say is 'not now'.

"Your other child is a girl. I feel I have something trapped in me. She can't express herself. She's heaven but trapped inside her body. She's an old, old soul and communicates through her eyes." That's when the tears came. I had been having such a hard time with my eldest for six months, since she had been told about her father's girlfriend on the eve of her 13th birthday, and cried herself to sleep in my arms two nights in a row, as we listened to Gabrielle – the CD I had listened to during her birth. For months I had been saying she was suffering. I could see it in her eyes. She never shared her feelings. Instead she had erected a wall around her. And it was tearing me apart. So the reassurance that followed filled my body with strength, knowing that she would be okay. And looking back I chuckled as I typed, remembering my psychic say that she would become a psychologist, as she had just chosen psychology A Level (without my interference; she's fiercely independent and chose her A's without hardly any consultation with her parents). And she wants to explore a degree in Psychology or Marine Biology! Wow, how could she know then that my daughter would go on to study (Marine) Biology 6 years later. "Please let go of any guilt you are holding on to" I was warmly instructed.

The medium went on to describe my ex-husband. As if she had known him for years. I had told her nothing about him or our separation. And she proceeded to describe it all perfectly. Reiterating things I had thought to myself but not heard from anyone (except a little from my white witch friend on the hill). Giving me the okay to feel hurt and upset by his action. Confirming his fear of emotion. His prioritising work over family. Reassuring me I hadn't done anything wrong. "He's done you a favour because you can now concentrate on how you want to live your life". Permission to live the life I desired. A sigh. A softening of the shoulders.

She came back to me. "You have an artistic side you haven't used for years; you might want to open to your creative side so you can be more like you. It's part of you and who you are. Don't deny it. If you want to paint your lounge orange do it." I laughed as I had been choosing colours to paint the chimney breast, to slowly get rid of the feeling of 'our' home and make it 'my' home. Not with anger, rather with self-love and playfulness.

"There's someone coming in, who is younger than you who has come here to heal you to remind you of what you have shut away and make you feel confident and get you back on the road. Enjoy it. Don't stress about it." Well, I won't divulge too much about that, but boy was she right. And I did enjoy it. Girls, allow yourselves to have fun. To feel attractive, sensual, desired, whether you are a mother of three or not.

Finally, before the hour was up the medium said she had felt she needed to share what the guides were communicating about me, but that now a spirit had come to the front. I know who she was and she came to explain a little about my mum. But that's for the next book.

Then another spirit came forward. To be honest I still haven't been able to pinpoint who the lady that was described is, but her message was clear; "you are not judgmental, you are open and interested and you wouldn't judge anyone about how they have behaved." Words that have popped up in my life just this week again. Words that explain why, despite the behaviour that broke my heart time and time again, and eventually my soul, I have been able to forgive. As I have learnt, and share time and time again, we can only use the skills we have at the time.

When someone hurts you, it's all about them, where they are, not about you. Remember that; it gives you the strength to get up off the floor and rebuild your life. You are brilliant, bright and beautiful. Whole, perfect and complete.

So that was my first session with my medium 7 years ago. I had gone in with no expectation. Just a desire for some guidance. A helping hand about what next? It is exhausting to receive so many messages, and as I drove away I wanted to go home and sleep. But I felt that out there people were watching over me. That there was a path I was on, one that was meant for me. Even though the last 8 years had been painful, I felt it was all for a reason. I understood that each person comes into our lives for a reason. That relationships teach us things about ourselves, so that we can be stronger and more able to cope with the next lesson.

I have been to see that medium at least annually since. Each time spirits have come forward to guide me. Totally unexpected ones. The messages of the second session just 3 months after the first, were just as clear and incredibly encouraging. If like me you have lost the love of your life and are trying to move on and start again towards a life you desire, it is helpful to hear that you must give yourself permission to find a new love, that you deserve one.

Someone who will give you the space you need to be you. Or if, like me, you have started something like I started writing this book 7 years ago, and aren't sure if it's the right thing or going in the right direction, it is reassuring to know they will help your words flow, help fill in any gaps, so that you can create something that will be informative and help others heal.

Then I got busy training to teach Mindfulness to 4-to-11 year-olds, starting with an online course from the USA. Soon after that I completed the MiSP paws.b training and before I knew it (well actually as a result of emailing 50 schools in a 5 mile radius), was hired by two excellent independent schools on my doorstep to teach my first courses. By January 2016 I had taught 8 classes of 24 children, each lesson boosting my confidence and filling me with gratitude that I was finally leading the work life I desired.

Aware that there had been a huge shift in my life, I returned to the medium for a third session of guidance in January 2016, conscious that while my Mindfulness teaching career was blossoming, my book remained unwritten, my bank account remained low ... and my bed and heart remained empty. I was curious to know how to focus my energy on improving those three areas. Guides came instantly. Interesting messages about this book. "In this new phase will come opportunity for you to work more, to do with research and bringing together a lot of information for a book, pulling together all the bits for work, it will come to you, they will help you and this will lead to work". Confusion, as until then I had focussed on an autobiography, and was finding it hard to progress. But the idea that my exploration of different life experiences was actually research for a book intrigued me. "It will lead to you feeling better about yourself, stop feeling you should have done things differently, stop beating yourself up, it was all part of the fabric of your life, it was all meant to happen, stop the what if's". I felt a new energy to sit and type and live and sit and type.

Then there was the question of my slightly lonely heart. "You needed to be like this, you needed to be on your own, you would have always felt too comfy with him, you will realise you can thank him because you are in a much better place. Be strong. Do the book". To be honest I was sure about the book already and wanted more guidance on love, so the next message was a little hard. "I feel you don't really want someone in your life. You need to align your head and your heart. Opportunities have come your way but you haven't wanted them". Mmm. True. But a girl has to have her standards. "What you need isn't always wrapped in the packaging you are imagining. Be more patient with people coming in". Oh okay, maybe I need to lower my standards? If, like me, you have been hurt more than once, you sure ain't willing to let any old riff raff into your heart. But to hear that maybe you are being TOO picky can be useful too. "You haven't had someone to look after you and you can have that. You will get someone solid who won't restrict you. They will come if you allow them." Getting orders from a higher plane to allow someone in. Who can argue with that? I wasn't about to. And thanks to my Mindfulness practice and my nourishing work, I was in a place where I could heed the guidance and find the patience and trust to know love would come, but also was grounded enough to accept that maybe I had been shutting love out because starting something new, would mean accepting the end of something old.

Anyway, with a new slant to my book and orders to let love

in, life got even busier. Another two top independent London schools hired me to teach in 2017, as well as a state one and my first schools asked me back for a second year. By Christmas I had taught 1500 more students and taken another big step on my journey; I trained to teach adults MBCT. I was feeling alive and knew it, as JKZ said. I loved my work and knew it was making a difference. So, 14 months passed until I went back for a fourth session, forever keen to make sure I was on the right path, in the right way (and by now more than curious about when love would come). In that session the guides reiterated the message that my purpose on this plane is to communicate. And despite being busy teaching, when cash is tight and the voices creep in that maybe it's time to give up on what feels right and go back to what paid well,

> *guidance that what you are doing has always been your path, gives you the strength to keep on doing what you know in your heart is right.*

To hear that you have forgotten your self-worth and that you ARE important because you listen to others, boosts your confidence and gives you the courage to explore new ways of getting your message out. It's a win-win situation. And if like me you have felt guilty for having big dreams, for planning retreats in wonderful locations just because you want to, because you desire it, then to hear a soul who knew you when you were ten tell you to "wish big and don't be afraid to dream big and have big ambitions", helps you lift your head up high and know you have made the right choices. The choices that are true to you. That will lead you to live the true authentic life you desire.

The first four sessions had helped me gain confidence about my chosen path and my imminent love. But my finances were a mess. Although I was great at getting new contracts, teaching Mindfulness wasn't going to afford me financial freedom exponentially. I had invested a small fortune in no less than five Mindfulness courses, plus the compulsory silent retreat and monthly supervision that come with being an MBCT teacher. And the odd trip with the children to keep my wanderlust satisfied. As a true indecisive Libran, always wanting to give things one more go, keen to find a solution, I had um-ed and ah-ed about the house in Portugal (which wasn't actually mine, just a drain on my finances) and so the next guide surprised both my medium and myself. "This is odd" she started. "Never happened before. I have another guide here. He's your finances guide. He wants you to get your money into one pot so that it can work for YOU". That was all I needed to hear to know that, while my resourceful, creative self had kept things floating for years, it was time to try a new tactic, without feeling any shame. My conviction was hardened to do whatever I needed to cut ties, cut losses and start afresh. To lead the financial life I desired.

The same message came through again about finally focusing on MY heart. If, like me, you have spent years trying to please others, worrying they won't get by without you, that's bullshit. We owe nothing to anyone except to ourselves. Before we met anyone, we arrived in this world with OUR lives to live. Our purpose. Our needs and wants. So to hear from a soul that knew me AND him well, that I was trying to help him learn from his mistakes, to stop him from preventing more, but that it was time to LET GO, filled my heart with warmth ... and permission. To be told categorically to do things for ME, that I had permission to prevent myself from ending up lonely, felt like the hug I still needed to finally cut the emotional ties I had. "Your head is telling you you have moved on, but you need to tell your soul that your heart has moved on too." So seven years almost to the day from our first separation, the guides from another place gave me the confidence and reassurance that it was time for me to focus my attention on ME. To lead the life my heart desired. And so I filed for divorce. I had waited for him to do it, but true to form he hadn't got around to it. What would have been impossible for me before the 8-week MBSR course, came with great ease, as I filled in form after form that would allow me the space to move on, feeling supported by a whole community of guides watching over my left shoulder. And I really encourage you to keep an open mind and open your ears to the guidance that is there for you … you just have to ask for it.

Step 8. Get out, get creative and get surprised!

One of the many advantages of being a single mum on a mission of self-rediscovery, who has 13 weeks holiday a year as a teacher and time-shares her kids with their father, is that I get two whole weeks off a year, just for me, in the glorious summer months, while they travelled with him to their grandfather's house in Cornwall or to his boat in Turkey. Not a bad life for them either – another good thing that came from our marriage. So, over the last years I have tried different ways of making the most of those two weeks, some more successful than others. More self-loving than others. The first few attempts were before my MBSR course and were either fun or self-flagellating, as I tried out different options. Then when the Mindfulness penny had dropped they took on a new energy. A new sense of direction.

The first time I had found myself with seven whole days on my hands, I foolishly used that time to declutter, spring clean, sort, fix … generally pootle about, looking after the house by day and meeting with friends in the evening. Black and decker by day and bubbly by night. Charity shops then chattering chops. Clearing then clubbing (I could go on, I do love a bit of alliteration).

So, the second year I decided to have more fun and get out of London. One afternoon I was packing the kids' cases for their Cornish capers while chatting to my brother, who happened to be in London from LA. I happened to think out loud that it would be great to leave London and enjoy my kid-free-ness with my generous younger brother, and within two days the Universe answered and I was on a plane with him and a friend of his, on the way to Ibiza, no less. Spontaneous doesn't begin to describe how it felt. Luckily, I had been going to the gym since finishing the PGCE a month earlier, so I was reasonably beach-body ready (nowadays I don't care as much about my outer appearance, as I am so much happier with what's inside). In true Ibiza style, we spent four days taking advantage of everything the paradise has to offer; designer villa with pool, 3 nights of clubbing 'til 9am and 3 days of people-watching on the beach beside crystalline waters. And there was no shortage of people to watch. I had never seen such large male muscles squeezed into such small fluorescent speedos, as groups of young people paraded up and down the beach, advertising that night's event in the many renown clubs on the party island, all clad in eye-catching, revealing beachwear that made your eyes goggle. Everywhere I looked, there were young Adonis's lying belly down, sleeping off the previous night's excesses, exposing their beautifully crafted shoulders and stunning geometric tattoos.

> *The abundance of carefree self-confidence around me was refreshing. There was no sign of guilt or responsibility. Just people allowing themselves to have a good time without overthinking things.*

I returned to London re-invigorated; it was okay to stop being a mum for a while.

Unfortunately, the following year wasn't quite as glamorous, as instead of picking up the high frequency vibes of island party-goers, I attempted to reconnect with my future-ex's family, joining them at their sandy solace by the Camel Estuary. Looking back now I find it interesting that earlier, when I had thought there was a chance of us getting back together, I was able to feel confident and be upbeat. However, having just completed an exhausting year as an NQT, under a bully of a boss in a nearby school, and having received the news that nailed the coffin shut about his new relationship, I didn't have the energy I'd had the previous year to contemplate partying the night away, as I had just 12 months earlier, G&T in hand, ankle deep in a warm water pool, surrounded by beautiful bodies and listening to party anthem after party anthem. No. Shaken by the news that my future ex had a girlfriend, I struggled to live so intensely among people I felt had shunned me in recent years and who in my opinion, had done little or nothing to help when our marriage had been so clearly screaming for it. I often think about that bit where the priest or registrar reminds the congregation at a wedding that, with the witnessing of the coming together of a couple, comes the commitment to be there for them should they ever need it. And I have often thought that the only people who ever offered to carry out that duty of care were my mother and my brother. The 31 other people at the wedding had until then never raised a hand of help. In what felt like true English fashion, the demise of our marriage was observed in silence from afar, receiving only criticism, not concern. Charity did not begin at this home.

Nevertheless, the pain and sleepless nights I endured that self-flagellating week were worth it, as the kids clearly enjoyed time spent as a family (as they still do whenever I conjure up family days) and given how much time their father spent at his laptop as was his habit, it was lucky I was there to keep my broken-toed, plaster-footed son company. The poor lad had been so happy to be able to run free after the 9-hour drive from London, that he hadn't seen the large rock covered in grass on the back lawn. He started his first day of the 6-week summer holiday in Truro hospital, praying his cast would come off by his birthday, so that he could speed around the Algarve karting race track as usual (and the universe did deliver his wish 4 weeks later).

As I now look back on that week, I see that it was a desperate attempt to hold onto something that had slipped through my fingers. A classic example of my tenacity in the face of the impossible. But one that was not driven by self-love or purpose, just fear and almost self-loathing. However, it was lovely to reconnect with some places and some people dear to my heart. But I wouldn't recommend it. I can now look back at the attached efforts of the old me with kindness rather than criticism and be grateful for how that person has grown. Has learnt. And that is done by making mistakes, often from a place of fear. The strongest piece of advice I can give anyone in the middle of a break up: love not fear.

The following year however made up for it 100%. Having completed the 8-week MBSR I was able to make decisions from a place of love. Flicking through the pages of my then favourite magazine – Psychologies – I had often seen an ad for Skyros. A whole page of Mediterranean blue sea with inset shots of smiling people around tables on patios with swathes of bougainvillea ... A holiday with a difference, it claimed. The best alternative holiday, according to The Guardian. As I explored the various workshops on offer, my eye was caught by a creative writing option. Having somewhat arrogantly decided that I was going to turn myself into a writer (I had visions of getting myself out of financial dire straits in a J.K.Rowling-esque way with Elizabeth Gilbert-esque success), I decided that this was the right next step to get closer to that goal. After quickly checking flight prices there (and wondering why certain airlines call themselves low-cost), I extracted my worn credit card from my Oliver Bonas taupe wallet with its bold, white A printed on the front, and typed in the 16-digit number.

The site's blurb offered "Europe's Leading Learning Holiday" and I was on a high-speed learning mission. "Adventure, creativity and joy! New skills, renewed self-confidence, a fresh outlook or even a whole new way forward" was promised and I wanted ALL of it. I landed in Athens and made my way to the city centre hotel to meet some of the other travellers, a little nervous. I was to share a room in a traditional Skyros house with a total stranger. Not something I was wild about but it was the cheapest option. She failed to turn up that night and I was a little relieved. The next day we took a coach to Skyros and I was quite quiet for the whole journey, slightly stunned by the bravery I was tapping into to actually be there. The views as we got off the dual carriage way in Athens were stunning. After A Levels, most of my friends had gone inter-railing, but as my then boyfriend refused to rough it, I had stupidly forsaken that rite of passage and never really forgiven myself for missing out. For letting a boyfriend and his allergy to public toilets, get in the way of an adventure of a lifetime. So, I tried to see the coastal and island views with a teenager's eyes, albeit from a coach full of self-discovering, sweet smelling 30-50 somethings, rather than a train full of sweaty youths.

When we arrived at the village I was mesmerised. The coach had to stop outside the village on the hilltop, and we dragged our cases up through the charming, narrow winding streets to the main building of our stay for the next week. A lovely couple explained the timings for 7am yoga, breakfast, workshops, lunch and free-time, as well as options of how to fill it. Then we were shown to our 'rooms'. Skyros houses are small. There is an upstairs family room and kitchen on one level, with a mezzanine area for sleeping, and a patio facing the sea, and steep stairs down to a bedroom with ensuite bathroom, with a window that opens up at pavement level. The upstairs room had already been taken by my roommate, who had arrived a day earlier, so I took the room downstairs. I was pleasantly pleased by the privacy the house offered. A proper retreat. I unpacked and went to supper, curious about who else had come to Greece to find themselves.

The next day we started the workshops. Our room was right next to the breakfast patio. It was a large rectangular room, with a large rectangular table in it. On one side a wall of glass offered views down the hill to the sea and blue, blue, sky. The 12 of us sat around the table with our coach, Deborah Levy, in the middle facing the windows. There was no schedule, no list of activities that we were going to follow. After briefly introducing ourselves and how much (or in my case how little) we had already written, Deborah gave us our first writing task. A Haiku. A Japanese style of poem, with seventeen syllables in three lines; 5, 7 and 5 syllables respectively. We were all relieved to start small! As we each read ours out, you could sense any shyness or embarrassment disappear, for the room was filled with palpable kindness, non-judgement and gentleness. The two hours passed in a flash. There was a vagueness to the session that was both disconcerting and empowering. What had been taught? What had been learnt? What had taken place in each of the twelve minds for those a hundred and twenty minutes? We were given homework to write material that afternoon to read out the next day. So after a chatty lunch we each went our separate ways; some choosing a stroll to the beach, some a walk through the village and others a nap. The fluidity and lack of responsibility was refreshing.

And so the week unfolded. The writing tasks got longer, more specific and more personal. One about our most memorable event, where one fellow aspiring writer recounted a dive in a Blue Hole where he had come face to face with near-drowning and nose-to-nose with a shark! One day we had to write our homework on something found in the village; I scoured the beach that day and came across three large stones, and wrote a letter to each of my children on them. And the finale pushed us out of our comfort zone (well some of us, anyway); a fictional piece involving sensuality and sex, which each of us explored in such varying ways, that I was totally taken aback by how one task can be interpreted so differently by twelve humans. And by how a sweet looking person, can write pure filth! There were stories of raunchy housewives philandering with tennis coaches, teenagers being accosted by strangers in the back of taxis, and school girls daydreaming about affairs with their teachers. After just five days we had matured as writers and grown as individuals. It was truly wonderful.

But Skyros offered so much more than just writing skills. The twelve people around that table each had a tale to tell of suffering and survival; of divorce, death, illness, loss, abuse and suffering. Those stories weren't shared as tasks; they just made their way out into the open organically as the group came together in that room overlooking the Med. There were the stories that we wrote down for Deborah, but these were just a step in a process to find the voice and the words to tell the stories we had lived and felt in our broken hearts. Some would come to print. Others would remain in diaries and in piles and piles of typed sheets on the floor. Each story touched me and I came away feeling blessed to have met such brave and beautifully vulnerable souls. I would recommend a writing workshop to anyone wanting to get to know and understand themselves better, whether you want to be published or not.

However, more than writing techniques and memories of wonderful people, what Skyros gave me were two precious things I had not expected. One was a message I still carry with me on a daily basis. One day early in the week Deborah came up to me in a break. We hadn't spoken too much on a personal level. But she sat down next to me on the steps overlooking the sea, looked into my eyes and said:

"you don't have to be responsible for everything, for everyone."

It was as if she had looked beyond my pupils and into my heart, my soul. How could she know how I felt? The weight I felt to 'look after' my mother, my brother, my children and even the man who had broken my heart? But I received her permission to 'just be' unquestioned. I trusted that those words had been said to me for a reason and with good intention. With compassion. We didn't discuss her advice much more and soon moved onto talking about the book I wanted to write. When I shared that I wasn't sure where to start, she simply offered 'start where you like', words I have also repeated to myself time and time again over the last seven years. Start where you like. Why not try it too?

Writing skills. Heart-warming connections. Priceless words of advice. I had gone to Greece expecting just the former. In addition to bonuses already mentioned I received one more; a friend for life. Without explanation over the week Jessie and I came together and by the end of the 5 days were inseparable, spending afternoons at the beach together, eating dinner together, and taking moonlit walks along the sand. We laughed those 5 days away and shared our stories in the privacy of just our ears. Holiday friendships often fade once you come back home. Maybe you meet up once or twice then as time passes the reunions get fewer and further apart until all that is left is a text on birthdays and a Christmas card. This friendship however has lasted. Luckily we live in the same city, which has probably helped. Over the last seven years what started on a small Island in Greece has grown into a beautiful friendship which thrives on humour, lack of judgement and support. They didn't write that in the ad, did they!

So, whatever creative 'hobby' or pastime you enjoy, whether it's writing or painting or pottery or something active, go do it! Find a workshop, or course or retreat or holiday, and get out of your comfort zone. Meet new people. Make new friends. You deserve it. And your soul needs it.

Step 9: Get un-blocked: release your abundance

Summer 2015 the energy was high and the urge for growth and development even higher. I was determined to tackle my future from all angles. There is something energising about having to rebuild your life unexpectedly. Something good does comes out of it (eventually). The short burst of writing in February had spurred me on to explore further my talents as a writer. Partly because I enjoyed it and partly, tbh, because I was desperate to try anything to increase my financial abundance – after all, it had worked for JK (although luckily, I wasn't on benefits). Having already booked myself onto the Skyros writers' course for July, as well as the MiSP (Mindfulness in Schools Project) 'paws.b' teacher training course for August (both conveniently in weeks when I would be kid-free; confirmation that they were meant to be), I came across a programme on the fab Mindvalley.com, which promised to help me "Break Free From The 24 Abundance Blocks Keeping Me From A Life Of Affluence & Contribution". So,

I went for a triple whammy. I had already listened to the ninety-minute free workshop by the legendary healer, Christie Marie Sheldon, and had heard things that made sense to me in my new intuitive state. The course also offered me my money back if I wasn't satisfied that it had helped me 'eliminate energy blocks, raise vibrations and manifest ideal realities'; I had nothing to lose (except 24 hours)! So I paid the few hundred dollars willingly, determined to complete it over the summer …

Three whole months later I logged on for the first time (hey, no judging! It had been a busy summer.). Session one: 'Clearing Resistance' – seemed easy enough, I thought. After all I had chosen to do the course (and Christie thanked us often for 'showing up'), so I felt no resistance was there. The first thing I was asked was where I wanted to be in twelve weeks' time? Mm, I thought. Having felt as a child that I had everything I needed, I wasn't used to asking for much (and the things I had expected – diamond ring, anniversary gifts, flowers – had never materialised, so I was used to not getting those unspoken desires either). Now I was keen to push the boat out. Dare I ask for it all; a new communicative and passionate soulmate, a diary filled with work to enable me to pay school fees, buy a bigger house, AND travel anywhere I wanted (Christmas somewhere hot and sunny sprung to mind)? And the motivation to finally write a life-changing novel? "Don't feel guilt or shame, as they block you" the audio encouraged. So I went to town and asked for it ALL.

That was the easy bit – asking for it all (and it wasn't even Christmas!). Next came a flood of advice about how to manifest these desires. I listened attentively as I was told that fear, anger, shame, defeat and worry are low energy thoughts that have a blocking effect. Damn it! That explained my slow decline from earning a decent salary a dozen years earlier, to hovering around a figure a third of that for a decade, as I tried and failed and tried again to find work that fulfilled me. I had felt shame at leaving the stability of the well-paid job at the bank to become a self-employed interior designer. Shame at the meagre revenue generated during those 8 years. And defeat when projects didn't all go well. I felt shame again when I abandoned that to retrain as a teacher, leaving the house at 8am and not returning until after 6pm, while my children were shunted from pillar to post, only to have to rush them into bed quickly in order to sit down and study or prepare lessons in the evening. But those were nothing compared to the anger I had felt for years as my husband failed to respond to my incessant pleas to share with me what was troubling him. My response to his withdrawal looked like anger and bitterness, but that was just its outward manifestation; beneath that I was hurt, lonely and scared. Really scared that he was slipping away and that there was nothing he was letting me do about it …

Instead of these negative, blocking feelings the guru encouraged us to feel love, peace, joy, fun and playfulness. Sounded great. Then came the clanger – I would have to not only show my and others' past baggage, but embrace it, so that I might release it. OK, so unlimited abundance was going to come with some hard work. Mm. I had kind of hoped all the baggage I had faced over the previous year would have been sufficient self-exploration. That this would be merely forward looking. But I remained open-minded, if not a little wary.

Next we were asked to list what blocked us. As the audio was a recording of live sessions I could hear what the original attendees had listed without having to reveal my own. I felt at a slightly voyeuristic advantage and was intrigued as I heard their blocks: only others make money, hard work is never enough, wanting money is greedy, I'm not worth it. There was some reassurance in hearing that I wasn't alone in my pessimism. But then the sage began to empower her audience. Even though I wasn't part of the online live group, I could feel the energy that she was raising with her bold instructions. I was being ordered to show I was enough just as I was (in my pj's on my bed), that I shouldn't do things to please others (watch out people), I shouldn't follow the rules (it was getting better and better) and think outside the box. Luckily there is a strong roof on my house, otherwise, like Alice, I might have ended up outside said box, as my confidence grew so large, it burst out of the Velux windows above my head.

It struck me that perhaps this was the voice of a father – motivating words that should have been heard while growing up, urging me to do and be whatever I wanted, without boundaries or limitations. Without fear, just courage and gusto, ready to take on the world? I liked to think those were the messages I had already passed on to my 3 children, but struggled to recall a memory of them having been said to me, however hard I used my Hippocampus!

So I fell asleep that night with a long list of promises to myself; I would make choices that were loving and kind TO ME; I wouldn't beat myself up and blame myself; I would have FUN. And whenever an old niggle would creep into my head, I would laugh at myself and say 'doh! How can you still be bothered about that silly old thing?'. But some promises were scary and seemed out of my reach – I made a vow to let go of the belief that my marriage should have lasted forever, and instead told myself an even better future lay ahead ....

The course recommends that you hear each session at least twice and manifest your desires 30 to 40 times a day. While I didn't quite meet the targets, I was focussed enough to dedicate a little time each day to my desired future – being stuck in early morning traffic for 20 minutes each morning as I drove to the kids' school bus and back became a very productive part of my daily routine! To my astonishment within just two weeks I had secured not one, but two new contracts as a Mindfulness teacher, each offering me the daily rate I had manifested in that first hour of listening. The Universe works in wondrous ways, I have no doubt about it. I was on a roll and soon settled down to Session Two: Clearing Doubt and Fear.

Eagerly I listened as it explained that realities are created with several things in mind. First of all we can re-energise things if we openly hold them dear to us. Basically I was being told that my inner thoughts of what was important for me, had the power to be reflected in or create the world I live in. Now I know this is true as it has happened so often to me, but then it was a new (and slightly scary) idea for me, as someone who had lived in her head with non-stop thoughts since primary school. It was even suggested that merely hearing others' ideas and taking them on as our own was enough. For those of us who thought money was bad, she asked if our parents had told us that or if it came from us? Indeed being raised on a council estate by a waitress had led me to believe that only others have large houses and lots of money. But as I never once was encouraged to earn lots so that

I could live elsewhere, I didn't ever entertain the thought that I would smash through salary ceilings like Charlie in his elevator. I remembered that during the last year of university, as many of my friends were attending 'milk rounds' and exploring which banks or consultancies they wanted to work for, I hadn't been interested at all. That world (or the little I knew of it) seemed boring to me. Ironic, given where I would end up before the end of the millennium. And now I was being told that as I had never held money dear to me, it hadn't shown up - the bankers were right after all!

So I listed half a dozen things that I hold dear to me. The next concept presented was that things turn up for us in the future according to what we say today and I was warned not to say things unless I was sure I wanted them! I began to feel dread as I remembered the times I had criticised my husband, when actually I was just angry and was trying to goad him into reacting. All I wanted to hear was 'shut up you old hag, don't you know I love you'. My despair at his years of silence had led me to say things I didn't mean and now they had turned into reality. I had even asked for a divorce when what I really wanted was a hug and a declaration of love. But then my ego was controlling my mouth and my ego had been hurt, really hurt. So, promise to self, never say something if you don't mean it.

The third idea was that where and how we direct our vibrations or energy now, is where and how our energy will be in future and she guided us to be wary of others' negative energy, which is strong enough to make you sick (nowadays I keep well clear of such people and haven't been ill for ages). I was encouraged to live each day as if I was already in the life I wanted. It was beginning to feel like I was learning to act on stage, something that had always scared my pants off! But now it seemed like a fun idea – willingly I imagined myself as a sought-after teacher with my diary FULL of Mindfulness teaching, and a published author signing books in Waterstones, living in a big house by the common and shooting off all over the globe, showing the world's wonders to my children (NY, the Alps and Safari, I knew exactly where I wanted to go).

Finally, our teacher maintained that our reality is created by listening to ourselves and rearranging what we do to align with our true intentions, so that the universe gets clear signals about what we want. Again I recalled in horror the fickle way I had spent the last five years oscillating from steely determination that the road ahead alone was the best one, to sad regret about our breakup, and back to positivity about a new life, a new love. No wonder my new Mr Right hadn't turned up – the poor Universe must have been dizzy with my indecision. OK. Enough.

After a fairly soft start to the course, I was beginning to feel heavy but then she lifted us up and showed us how to unblock this doubt that I and many others had. The cure seemed easy: don't neglect yourself (walk away from the wine), embrace change (dating can be fun, right?), do things that make you grow (brownie points here – 3 courses already, get me!), love yourself ("I am whole, perfect and complete, I am whole perfect and complete"), bring old unconscious messages to the fore (why did Dad leave, then my husband? It's NOT okay) ... then blow them all up! I was being urged to follow my inner guidance whole heartedly, see my book on the shelf, see the new (younger) man by my side, enjoy my weirdness! Know I AM good enough.

I certainly had work to do that week: in order to help my abundance I would have to change my energy, unblock my knowledge, stop avoiding things. What was I avoiding she asked? Good question. Hard question. Despite being perfectly happy to stand up in front of hundreds of colleagues or parents, presenting about tried and tested ideas and practices, I suddenly realised that I might be avoiding mastery – I was shying away from standing out in the crowd and shouting out about my passion - Mindfulness. That was fairly easy to embrace. Much harder was the self-confession that I was avoiding the pain of admitting my husband loved someone else now. That stung a little. I knew I was avoiding divorce but that was a paper process. This was more. And I guess I was even avoiding getting out there to meet my new Mr Right, by always going for people that clearly could only be Mr Wrong … Sound familiar?

Doubt on its way out, I would have to focus on neglect too and only spend time and effort on things and people that work for me and my abundance. On a good note, I knew it wasn't laziness getting in the way, but despite the Mindfulness, I was still talking to myself a little (who doesn't?) which I was told decreases your energy. Oops. That would account for the motivation dips I had experienced over the last year – one day feeling on top of the world and the next day shrouded in heavy, inexplicable lethargy, that appeared out of the blue (like those extra pounds on the scale). So, my promises to myself that night included to do things for myself from a place of compassion: drink more water and less wine, take on less projects and put myself before my children and my mother …

So much in just two sessions, but three and four were a lot easier on the soul. We concentrated on unblocking the fear of change and I was surprised to realise I wasn't as fearless as I had thought. I was determined to write but worried of what others might think when they read my story. Would they think I was bonkers? Pity me? Criticise me? I had also prided myself at getting things done, but when it came to the book, I suddenly discovered a love for hoovering, laundry and dishes. Funny that. Procrastination was new to me. I knew I had to find a new kind of energy, a new driving force. I had to let go of the belief that it was safer to be small and be confident in being myself, warts and all. I had to let go of the guilt I felt about putting the man I loved down, let go of the hurt and pain he caused me. Let go. To help me move forward I had to create a new energy – one that generated financial freedom in a way I could be proud of. After all, the feeling when thinking about the book and when writing it felt light, so it must be TRUE.

Four hours into my quest for unlimited abundance I found a new version of myself ...With still 20 hours to go.

We then moved on to clear fear of growth. I had heard the phrase 'planting seeds' before used about mentioning something to someone, like a seed which will grow in them until they are ready to embrace it. Now I was being encouraged to allow my abundance to grow by planting seeds in a visualised garden, using meditation, something I was very comfortable with. But first I had to figure out which seeds I wanted to plant, in terms of the life I wanted, the love I wanted and the amount of money I wanted. Then I could fill this imaginary garden with love, light and abundance to get the future I so desperately wanted. As I sat and looked into the future, eyes closed, I envisioned all the things

I desired, some soulful, some materialistic; a successful business and published book, plenty of money to live in a modern house, drive a big shiny car, pay the school fees and travel the world with my children, to continue to go on courses and explore India and Tibet, a busy social life with endless invitations to dinner parties, my mother pain-free and of course a passionate life companion by my side. Once I had a clear image of my desired future, I set about choosing affirmations. First, ones that represented how I wanted to look at the world; to live life gratefully, to see the good in everything and to live life fully, passionately. Then affirmations about how I would share love in our world; by being kind to myself every day, by teaching others not to judge themselves and by being more mindful with my family. With the seeds for these desires clearly planted in my garden, I set about manifesting; repeating energy statements whenever I remembered, to raise my energy and create the life I desired. In the car, in the shower, in bed. A manic fest of abundance. It might sound crazy to any sceptics out there, but try it. Our mind, mood and energy respond to our thoughts and words. By repeating these energy raising statements to yourself, you can really change how you feel and how you act. And how the world acts with you.

Once you have designed your future garden, you just need to make sure you stay on top of the 'gardening'. Vision boards have been around for ages. I made one then and when I moved house recently I came across it and smiled; most of the things I put on it seven years ago, became my reality. I cultivated my garden, connected to the energy out there, tended to my dreams and my desires and many of the plants have grown. There are still things that haven't quite flourished yet, but I know they will come, when the time is right. By stopping to think about what I wanted, I gained a really clear understanding of what my life purpose was, which unlocked doors to making me happy. Something that had seemed unconceivable a year earlier. As I clarified the monetary desires I had, while deepening my sense of connection and spirituality, my garden became more and more abundant. I loved my work. In 2015 I had chosen a bold goal to bring Mindfulness to a million people, and three years later I was asked to work with an organisation whose motto is 'a million minds matter'. Coincidence? I think not. Give it a go – what do you want? Ask for it and see what happens. (See my tips on how to ask for it in Part Four).

By week seven I was completely comfortable asking the Universe for more than I had ever expected without feeling greedy. When old negative, blocking emotions popped up – life is too hard, am I worth it, bosses and husbands have hurt me - I uncreated them. Deleted them. I was learning to use tools that were shaping my life before my eyes. Of course there was hard work being done too. I dedicated time to approaching as many schools as I could, getting out of my comfort zone cold-calling head teachers to persuade them Mindfulness was the most important thing their school needed. And it started to work. Schools started calling me. In my first year of teaching Mindfulness I had delivered almost 30 courses and touched the lives of over 500 people. And it felt fantastic. Okay so I wasn't rich – yet – but my sense of purpose was enriching my soul. As my portfolio of meaningful career connections grew, I continued to focus on clearing any baggage I had, on freeing myself from old limitations. For the first time ever, I was making a mark in the world in a way that expressed who I was. I had previously enjoyed working in management development and in teaching, but this felt different. It felt truer to me and to how I wanted to be perceived. Some weeds had to be ripped out on the way; relationships that were sucking the energy from me were dug up. My garden was tidier and full of energy.

Once you allow yourself to accept you have fears, the rest becomes easier. I was learning more and more about mine, including some fears of rejection. And just like the Body Scan had taught me to connect with my body and sit with aches, breathe into them, breathe out from them, here I was beginning to understand how blocks to receiving love or money had manifested themselves in my body, explaining the aches I had had since June 2009, which I had previously put down to my heavy second baby! And the less we fear, the more space we have to express our true self; to do things that nourish our intellectual, emotional and physical self. Whether you decide to read more inspiring books, or workout more often, these choices are easier when you have let go of draining fears. And relationships become easier. A new kind of people started turning up in my life. Kind, connected, soulful people. My children even commented that I was happier, less grumpy. By embarking on a course to increase my financial wealth, I had opened the door to so much more. I was waking up full of energy and becoming at peace with the past. I was generating abundance.

To be honest some weeks I slipped. What should have taken six months, took a year. But there was no self-judgement, no self-blame. As and when I could, often on the treadmill, I continued to learn to clear my fears of money, of indecision, now that so many options were available to me. Together with my Mindfulness, the course was helping me notice if I was living from choice or reaction, from love or fear. I was able to keep a bold abundance goal in mind, without getting overwhelmed too often. Breathing, to be able to focus on each action step at a time. Overwhelm is something many of my course participants complain about. When the gap between where we are and where we want to be seems so huge and unbreachable, we can get scared and act from the fear. So it is important to stay grounded. To 'watch' the fear, without letting it hijack us. To trust that no gap is too wide. Over the last seven years many of the things I manifested have happened in ways different to how I had planned them. At the time I was aware of worrying about them but was able to remain curious and trusting of a positive outcome. And now in hindsight I can see how the Universe delivered my desires, just in its own way.

And to be honest some weeks I also felt stuck. Some weeks fears and blocks I thought I had cleared from my unconscious programming – about who was holding the strings to my life, or not being entitled to abundance - reduced my energy and broke my alignment to my goal. Luckily, thanks to my Mindfulness, I was in tune with my thoughts and feelings, and could identify any story I was telling myself that was negative or lacking patience, delete it and get back on track, directing more loving energy at my dreams and desires. Each week I was getting clearer about my values. And as I did, I learnt why I had done some of the things I had, that at the time had seemed irrational; pushing people away when others had suggested holding on, being stubborn when others had recommended flexibility. Previously I couldn't explain my actions, but now I was confident in the knowledge that I was just acting on my values, protecting them when others had threatened them. Which meant that along the way some things had to change to achieve the future aligned with the real me.

This new knowledge and confidence had a ripple effect. I found myself able to get over things more easily, no longer pondering incessantly on problems. The more connected and in tune I became with ME, the more powerful I felt to achieve my desires. I was becoming more and more open to new things, such as wacky bioenergetics, and saw opportunities everywhere, whether it was to train to teach a charity parenting programme, or climb a mountain in Africa. I was driven, inspired, motivated. Even as I write this and recall the feelings I had then, I can feel the blood racing through my veins, and the gratitude in my heart for having found that energy, after so many months, years even, of low vibration. One of the things that gave me that energy was clearing clutter. Whether it was money, emails or emotions, I was on full declutter mode. Releasing blocks and allowing the weight to melt from my shoulders. Letting go of being responsible, as Deborah had suggested earlier. Some attempts failed initially, for sure. For example, money came that slipped through my fingers. But each mistake taught me a lesson about myself that would serve me for the future. By doing some pretty serious soul searching and being really honest about my weaknesses and downfalls, I was able to grow.

One thing that kept coming up time and time again, and still does if I am totally honest, was my family. Things I had heard, absorbed, taken on as mine at an early age, were still blocking me. Why was I so desperate to have a big house? Was it because my mother had driven us past a house she wanted on the drive home from school and pointed it out every day? Why was I still entertaining the idea that abundance was for others? Was it because I had lived in a council flat while school friends lived in big houses? Why did I think I was worth less than others? Was it because I had sensed that my brother was loved more that I was? Did I think things would simply come to me, just as my school assisted place and free school trips had? Although it is easy for you to convince your mind that you don't believe these things, persuading your heart is a lot harder. And you need your heart on board to achieve big dreams.

Over half way through my journey to unblocking my abundance, the topic of blame came up. Abundance thrives on a special energy and patterns of blame can take you off your path. By blaming others for our situation we give our power to them. I could say it isn't my fault I crave attachment and can appear needy; the people who left me unexpectedly did that. Or, it isn't my fault I blocked wealth out; I was raised to believe money isn't important. But those thought patterns disempowered me. So, all I had to do was delete the patterns. Not assume the blame myself. Just stop subconsciously blaming others. Brene Brown has written some great books on blame, shame and vulnerability and the effect on young people. The good news is only 25% of our feelings of blame and shame come from our parenting, so we can use our 75% of the control to take full responsibility for the future we create. We can take charge. The first step is awareness. Although I had never consciously felt resentment for the things that were lacking in my childhood, unconsciously I had wanted this to be different.

> *As I looked into myself through the eyes of my*
> *inner child, I allowed myself to feel sad and even*

cross, and once I acknowledged those feelings,
they melted away.

When you know someone you love has done the best they could for you, it feels mean to want more. But in my experience it's ok to admit you wanted more. To allow yourself permission to have wanted more. And in that confession you gain knowledge about yourself, your hidden thoughts. Knowledge that enables you to create your reality, your way, without feeling guilty that you want MORE. The more you have, the more you can give to others who need it.

So just sixteen hours into this journey to getting the life I desired, I was discovering the ultimate me. I had found a level of self-love in the Church almost two years earlier but now I was taking it to another level. I could see myself blogging, writing, designing courses, teaching in schools and businesses. I even started writing my own Mindfulness-based intuitive life coaching programme, which I started a couple of years later. I could see myself in a new house, with a new man, travelling the world with my children. And I was putting in the work to figure out which personality traits I needed to catch up with this new abundance and which I had to let go of. People have often praised me for reinventing myself; from trainer, to interior designer, to teacher, to Mindfulness coach. Those reinventions had happened effortlessly and had brought me closer to my true self. But this reinvention, this transformation, to achieve the life I desired, was different. It was driven by self-awareness, brave vision and burning passion. And those three things had only come to me because I had fallen to the kitchen floor and put in the work to get back up again.

The great thing about deciding to go for maximum abundance is that once you start feeling the love, the energy, it is self-fulfilling. The more you focus on generating a new future you, the easier it is to stay positive. Some of the things I knew I had to do to make the shift, scared me shitless. Record my meditations, make videos for social media, write articles and actually post them. Offer to coach people so they too could begin to lead the life they desired. Who did I think I was? But each time I stepped out of my comfort zone, I released another chain of events in my favour. People started offering to help me, unsolicited. Recommendations increased. Invoices were paid earlier. We owe it to the planet to stop playing safe by playing small. If all seven billion of us could raise our vibrations, imagine what the world would feel like? So if you have a roof over your head, food in your fridge and your breath in your chest, you too can generate a future that is better for you and for OTHERS. Your abundance becomes their abundance.

So as you can see I went from feeling guilty about desiring wealth, to feeling obliged to use my gifts to create it. We all have a gift and we can all turn it into profit. By releasing any shame or guilt that had unknowingly kept me away from opportunities to grow, I was able to see myself as a business that would excel. I had created by future garden, and was getting really specific about the financial side of it. I knew I was creative and had good intentions in everything I did, but so far that hadn't been enough (apart from a year working in a bank).

> To have all my dreams come to fruition would take a new focus. More action. Less self-sabotage.

I had to be really honest with myself about financial decisions

I had made and was making, and at the same time use my intuition (we all have it!) to make choices that would lead to abundance. Luckily, once you have realised that the Universe has your back, and that you are loved unconditionally, you can handle huge amounts of truth and prevent further self-sabotage. You have the courage to look and learn. Empowerment, positivity and certainty become part of your fabric. You believe your self-worth and shut out anything that will stop you. As I was about to complete the last part of the course, I dipped once more into exploring the impact the love I had received (or not) as a child, was having on the flow of my finances and I literally filled any gaps by hugging myself more; more time with friends, more trips to places that nourished my soul, more dates. Learning is cyclical; you delve into something, learn, grow, change then come back to it again. I kept revisiting the issue of feeling loved or not, tending to old wounds, letting the light into the cracks.

How did the course end? Over the space of a year I had connected to the light, manifested, cleared fear, cleared feeling stuck, cleared lack of clarity and gained ownership for my sense of truth and my future. It was time to take massive bold action, without fear of messing up. It was time to go out into the world knowing I have a talent and a gift to give that will bring abundance. It would take investment, help and most importantly the courage not to care what others thought or said. It was time to align my outflow of money with my desired inflow of abundance. So slowly I started making bold decisions. Letting go of things that were draining me. Of ties I thought I needed to be safe. Contributing more to the world I live in without worrying about running out of time. I started a chain of events that are now coming to bear fruit.

Today doubts still creep in. My heart races at the thought of a drastically different future. But I check-in with my feelings daily, more often actually, and remind myself to act from love, not fear. With kindness and charity, not my ego. When I look at the vision board I created all those years ago, I smile, I feel blessed and I thank the Universe. What you focus on, you really do, eventually, create. Or rather what you desire is already there - you just need to get rid of whatever is blocking you from reaching it.

So please, if you are feeling stuck, trust that there is a way out and start somewhere. Whether you meditate, or go on a course, explore what is blocking you, do the work, and watch your abundance increase, guilt and shame free.

Step 10. Get high! Be on top of the world!

After the success of Skyros, I was determined to get away as much as possible and not let being single stop me do anything I had planned to do with my life. Morocco had been a place that we had toyed with visiting back in 2006, when we had decided to go further afield to Vietnam (which I REALLY recommend). So, I spoke with a friend who went there regularly and booked my flights mid-June for a week's stay mid-July (forever the last minute planner). I was keen to experience something a little different so, I booked four nights in Marrakesh, one of them in a rather special place, and three nights in the Atlas Mountains, where filming of stories set in 'Tibet' often took place, for their similarity to the Himalayas. As the departure date approached, I was petrified; what should I wear to be respectful of local customs? Would I be harassed? Was it safe to visit alone as a woman? A friend of mine reassured me that none of the above were cause for concern. But my heart raced as I packed the night before.

On arrival at Marrakesh airport, I took a taxi to the centre. I showed the address and map to the driver, who spoke almost no English, but nodded that he knew the location. When we got close, he stopped the taxi outside a labyrinth of small streets and said I was to walk the rest alone, as cars could not enter. My amygdala totally alerted, I was completely doubtful and suspicious, believing I was paying to be left in the middle of nowhere. A 'friendly' young man offered to show me the way to the Riad, which I gladly but somewhat naively accepted. He insisted on wheeling my bag there, and when we arrived (to my surprise exactly as he had promised) he asked for a tip for his help. I rudely declined, as much because I was still worried about being fleeced, as because I had no change. Once through the doors of the Riad however I began to relax a little. The tiny reception area opened out onto a typical atrium, with a blue-mosaic pool in the centre, surrounded by huge potted palms and other lofty plants. Just like on the website! All around the atrium wooden doors opened onto side rooms and a stair case rose to two further floors, each with a balcony overlooking the pool. I was shown to my room and left … to breathe. Phew. I had made it. I had flown alone to a Muslim country I had never been to, to one of the world's most densely packed cities, and made it safely to my room. In one piece and without having been robbed. My amygdala could rest now.

After changing into my swimming costume, believing tourists wouldn't dare wear bikinis in such a religious city, I walked up to the roof top patio, where there promised to be a bar to mingle, a pool to cool in and views to be swept away by. Immediately I was greeted by a couple of girls in their twenties in tiny bikinis like the ones I had left in London. Doh. At the bar I ordered a beer I didn't recognise and sat down to take it all in. I felt equally in awe of my bravery, as of the sea of roof tops before me, and I was quickly getting itchy to go out and discover this former imperial, walled city, with its world-famous mosques, palaces and gardens, and its maze-like alleys and thriving souks. "Prepare for your senses to be slapped" Lonely Planet warned. As I sipped my beer, I gained more and more courage to step out into the 'gateway to culture' for a right slapping.

Before setting off on my first expedition however my ears caught the conversation of the American couple beside me. Used to talking to strangers (which never ceases to embarrass my children) I interrupted and within minutes had found out that they were both divorced teachers from LA. We chatted about how they had met and what they taught and how they were enjoying Marrakesh. I was encouraged by the prospect of too finding love after my separation, and allowed myself a moment's day dream of future travels to wondrous places with my new soulmate. But then soon back to reality and to the reason I was there; to experience life in one of the world's most colourful, lively cities. With a map in my hand and a route in my mind, I stepped out of the safety of the Riad's walls and onto the slightly daunting streets of the neighbourhood just outside the Medina.

My heart raced as I followed the road beside the tall walls of the El Badii Palace (the ruins of the 16th century palace, funded by a ransom paid by the Portuguese!) to the centre, trying to walk confidently and look as if I had done it many times before. There were more people on the streets than when I had arrived, as the temperature was cooler. I followed the road beside the tall wall of the ancient palace until I reached the nearest gate into the Medina. Wide-eyed, I walked onto a large, open square, surrounded by shops and restaurants, and came across tourists sipping early evening drinks. Soothed by the familiar scenes, I began to relax even more. And then at the end of the next road, there it was. The Jemaa El-Fnaa square, brimming with sellers and food stalls. Locals, who heavily outnumbered tourists, filled the eateries. There were lights everywhere and familiar smells wafted in the air but with an intensity I had not known before. It had the energy of a funfair but looked like one, huge, bustling open air restaurant. It was amazing. Overwhelmed by the choice and worried that I wouldn't be able to communicate with the vendors, I picked a stall and queued, observing what local people were ordering. Picking something that looked delicious, I inched my way to the tables adjacent to the cooking pots, sitting down next to a family for some much-needed fuel. Afterwards, tired from my travels on high alert, I strolled a little more around the square then made my way back to the Riad. This time the streets were bustling with people on foot and on scooters, with tiny shops open along the way and mobile vendors dotted around. Apparently, Marrakesh lived by night but that night I had only the comfort and safety of my bed in mind, after so much excitement.

The next morning, after breakfast on the rooftop once more, I set off to explore the souks and one or two other landmarks. Unlike me, I had kept the itinerary loose, allowing for spontaneity (and the odd bit of misinformation about opening hours in the tourist guides). As I walked into Jemaa El-Fnaa again, I felt a new sense of confidence and was less tense in my shoulders. I spent the day strolling through the souks, daring myself to step inside the shops, despite knowing it would take me ages to extract myself after failing to haggle successfully. At each one the (male) owner would ask me where I was from, offering Spain or France as options. For some reason I decided that that holiday I would be Portuguese, which lit up their eyes, as they exclaimed joyfully "Ah, Ronaldo!". I strayed a little off my 'planned' route (if that is possible in a labyrinthine city) and ended up being shown around a maze of foul-smelling tanneries, where seas of pits dying leather sprawled out in front of me. Again, having naively misjudged the kindness of the 'guide', I insulted yet another local by refusing to pay a tip for my unsolicited tour (he had told me he was on the way there anyway). I had a mindful lunch overlooking the square, then set off for round two to visit the Ben Youssef Madrasa; an Islamic College from the 14th Century. The calm silence of the madrasa, with several tourists exploring its 130 student dormitories and shady courtyard, was a welcome escape from the afternoon heat. This was tourism as I knew it and I was able to relax totally, as I observed the carved inscriptions and patterns made from cedar, marble and stucco. On my way home I stopped for an early supper back in the main square and got talking to two young French girls I recognised from my Riad, again confirming that travelling alone didn't mean you had to be lonely abroad.

For my third day I decided to visit the modern part of town – Gueliz I walked the long, long road northwest from the Jamaa El Fnaa in the forty-degree heat, exploring the 12th century Koutoubia mosque and its gardens on the way, appalled at the slightness of the horses attached to carts, to show tourists around in the suffocating midday temperatures. At least they were resting in the shade, I told myself. Due to the intense heat, there were fewer people on the streets (just daft tourists). There was also the lush 18th century Cyber Park on my route, however despite its ornamental gardens with fountains everywhere, I wasn't particularly tempted to slow my pace down – I just wanted to reach my goal and get out of the sun. Even though I had let go of a packed schedule, I was still feeling target-driven. Somehow the modern architecture and cool, stylish appearance of the smart neighbourhood I was crossing, had revived a sense of urgency that the older, charming souks had kept at bay. Funny that. Is it easier to be mindful among traditional environments? Do modern places invoke modern mindlessness? I'm sure there is an element of truth in that. In fact, I was experiencing it. I crossed Place de la Liberte, trying to hold onto a feeling of freedom, as I explored the city in defiance of the heat, until I reached Plaza, the centre of Gueliz. I felt a slight sense of betrayal; I had left the charm of the souks and dedicated an afternoon to visiting its newer cousin, which offered Pizza Hut, KFC and McDonalds, instead of couscous and tagine. But it had been my choice, so I attempted to suspend judgement and regret and after lunch and purchasing a bikini for a roof top swim, I made my way back, still on foot through treacherous heat, to the safe hustle and bustle of the Jamaa El Fnaa. My last stop on the way was the 'ensemble artisanal'; a regulated, haggling-free closed market, where you could buy or just watch apprentices learning tradition crafts, offering items such as art, rugs, pots, instruments, slippers and poufs. Here every item was priced and you could browse without being harassed. I had found my kind of Marrakesh shopping experience! And left with a beautiful teal leather pouf that I admire daily in my living room in SW18! Back at the Riad, I rested my throbbing feet; the 5km return walk had felt like 20km under the July African sun. Still on a mission though to make the most of my Marrakesh adventure, after a short rest I was on my way back out for supper, when I bumped into the 2 French girls and we agreed to dine together at a restaurant in the Square and watch the Euro game together; France v. Portugal. The restaurant we chose had aircon, huge TVs on the wall and served beer! The atmosphere was gripping, as most spectators supported the French, which meant my celebration of the 1:0 victory for my home team was low key. That evening, dining with strangers, sipping beer in an exotic city, I felt like I was in my twenties again; carefree and roaming the world, as I had always sought to, I was coming back to what I had always loved; travel, meeting people randomly on the way, and seeing the wonderful places this earth has to offer. I felt alive and I knew it, with every nerve in my body.

The last night in Marrakesh was to be spent in a totally different location, a treat to myself ... an act of self-love; Riad Les Yeux Blues.

The boutique Riad is a breath-taking combination of contemporary and traditional styles. An absolute feast for the eyes. The staff were more welcoming and gentler than any I have ever met in my twenty years of staying at 5-star establishments all over the world. The decoration is beautiful and it offers not one but two pools; one on the cool ground floor, and one on the roof, surrounded by a variety of nooks to hang out in. I floated around in disbelief that I had brought myself to such a gorgeous retreat and booked a hammam experience, still keen to experience new things, to live. And boy did I feel alive. For those of you who have never had one (yet), a hammam is a cultural and religious traditional bathing experience, which uses water to bring pleasure (no surprise, given that the Marrakeshi came from the desert and so for them water was paradise). The cosy room was half lit and offered a spiritual element, not just a cleansing one, to bring my soul and my body into alignment. As I was washed and massaged with a series of natural oils, I began to relax (once I got over the intimate, tactile nature of the experience) and connect. Admittedly, to start with it felt a little odd to stand in front of a stranger half naked, both of us in silence, but after a while I just let each minute unfold and tried to suspend any comparison of this experience to any other massage I had had (although it felt a little similar to my cleansing on the hill two years earlier). Afterwards I decided that that day I wasn't going to brave the hustle and bustle energy of the Medina; I was going to stay retreated in this oasis, reflecting on the 3 wonderful days I had had, chilling in the pools, reading and writing. A self-imposed, unplanned silent retreat. For supper, I sat at a table for one beside the lower pool, on a floor of stunning hexagonal patterned tiles, surrounded by white arches and cedar carvings. It was blissful. But just as Marrakesh had offered chance meetings on each other night that week, that evening was no different. Next to me on another table for one sat a young lady from New York, who was stopping in Morocco on her way to meet a group of girlfriends in non-other than my heart-town; Lisbon! We chatted softly, comparing travel tales and I offered her a list of sights to see and places to eat on the next leg of her journey. It was the perfect end to a perfect day, before the life-changing experience I had no idea lay ahead of me.

My last morning in Marrakesh was spent mindfully eating the delicious breakfast offered by Les Yeux Bleus, before heading out on one final tourist visit to the Saadian Tombs. They are located to the south of the Medina and are one of the few magnificent remains from the dynasty of the same name that ruled from the early 16th century to the mid 17th century; Marrakesh's golden era. There I walked among peaceful gardens, amazed by the intricate symmetry of the mosaic walls in the many chambers at the burial site, which also included pretty gardens that wove around the tombs in contrasting asymmetry. It was a wonderfully calm end to an otherwise fairly busy four-day stay at this beautiful city that I couldn't believe I had taken so long to visit. A little sad, I collected my bag from the Riad, with its beauty and warmth and dragged it to the taxi ranks by the Sidi Mimoun bus terminal. Having asked where I could catch a shared minibus to Imlil, I waited leaning against the dusty wall, while minibus after minibus filled and left without inviting me onto it. Didn't these guys want my money? After what seemed like an eternity I was approached by a man in his fifties or early sixties and asked if I wanted a taxi. I looked at the row of shiny Mercedes in front of me and asked if he had air con? He confirmed he did and we agreed the price (I was less daunted by haggling by now) and I followed him to his cab. After one, two, three, four shiny cars, we got to his slightly more battered one, with air vents, and windows, rather than chilled aircon. Nevertheless, I was so grateful to be setting off after my longish wait and so keen to start the next part of my adventure, that I didn't let it bother me.

We spent the next hour and a half chatting, not without some surprising exchanges. He was keen for me to confirm that every single couple in the UK co-habited before marriage, something he seemed fairly envious of. And he told me he too was single, which I hoped wasn't a suggestion or offer …

The road was windy but after what felt like not much time at all we arrived 65km south of Marrakesh in Imlil; 1800m above sea level at the southwestern edge of the Atlas Mountains and at the foot of Jbel Toubkal – at 4167m high, the highest peak in North Africa and 29th highest in Africa. We struggled to find the Atlas Mazik Lodge but after a little asking around we located it just outside the centre of the village, not quite as accessible as the website had suggested. Maybe I was tired, or car sick, but I remember not being as compassionate as I usually am, as I had to trek over a stream along a muddy riverbank to reach the lodge, which was perched on a hill looking onto the mountains. I was even less open-minded when I was told that the 'kitchen was closed' but that they could cobble together a tagine for me to eat … in an hour and a half (you can't rush a tagine!) So, resigned to what was clearly out of my control, I went to my room and poured myself a drink I'd purchased in duty free 4 days earlier.

It was definitely Pimms o'clock. I set to confirming my guide for the next day's hike (one that had been recommended by an acquaintance in London) but was alarmed at the rate he was asking, which was a lot higher than I had been told. As tends to happen more and more in my life, just as I was asking myself and the Universe whether I should go with him anyway, I overheard German voices coming up the stairs from the only other guests at the lodge, whose room was half a flight down from mine.

Emboldened by the last four days' adventures, I walked barefoot to their room, knocked gently and enquired about their plans for the following day. They had a guide arranged for a much cheaper rate, in fact for a tenth of the price! So without any hesitation, I asked if I could join them and they agreed! Wow. Just like that I was going to climb a mountain with complete strangers twenty plus years younger than me! I cancelled my guide (who was more than just a little miffed), scoffed the freshly prepared tagine, which was well worth waiting for, packed my few things for the ascent and went to bed, slightly nervous.

With nothing more than a fleece, a headscarf, a headtorch, my iPhone and a Boots first aid kit, I joined Janina and Sinan at 9am at the meeting point with our guide. Ninety-three years after the first recorded Europeans climbed Jbel Toubkal, we purchased bottles of water and set off on the first leg of our 'non-technical yet moderately difficult hike'; a five hour walk to the refuge at 3207m. I was bemused to read afterwards, that the hike normally takes seven hours, as we did it in five, despite the temperatures soaring towards forty degrees at the start. I was impressed by my fitness level, as I found it easy to hike through the first village and past the floodplain and up into the valley, as it got steeper and bendier. We reached the refuge by around 2.30 or 3pm (having stopped for sandwiches made for us by the lodge). The refuge is a fancy-free collection of wooden cubes in the valley, housing five mixed dorms, each sleeping between eight and twenty-six people. I had flash-backs of a trip in South Africa ten years earlier, where we had shared a mixed dorm in a hostel outside Plettenburg Bay. Only this time there were no arms to hold me while I slept, to comfort me. So, still able to think on my feet despite tired legs, I asked if I could have the corner bunk closest to the door. That way I would only have to 'worry' about one side of me and could make a quick escape if need be. Janina took the bed next to mine and then Sinan was left in the third bed, potentially next to a stranger. I assumed that my young German companions were a couple (I would find out later they were just best friends) and that Sinan would protect Janina. As it turned out, not many nutters climb Toubkal in the July heat, so we were only joined by two other men that night; one from the north of England and one from Oz.

Having done little to no research about the hike and been told I needed nothing special by the guide, I rented a blanket for that night and went outside to stretch out and sunbathe on a bench, while our guide, and other guides, cooked our dinner. You guessed it – tagine. But it was like no other. Large barely chopped carrots and potatoes, not a nut or raisin in sight and large chunks of chicken. It was delicious. We were advised to go to sleep at 7pm as we would be woken at 2.30am for breakfast, before the final ascent to the peak for sunrise. As promised, we were alerted with moderate shouts in the middle of the night and having slept fully clothed, all we had to do was put our boots on and make our way to the dining room for coffee and toast with jam. It was pitch black outside. Lacking a head torch, the others were advised to use their iPhone torches to guide the way. A bit makeshift but better than nothing. I laugh now, as I think of the huge amount of kit purchased the following year for a planned 100 km walk across the South Downs, a much less treacherous walk, and am thankful that I had packed my headtorch, won in a Christmas lucky dip. So we set off, knowing it would take about 3 hours. Almost instantly, the slopes became not just steeper but incredibly slippery underfoot as we climbed the scree slopes, with our bodies almost parallel to the ground as we leant forward, scared to fall back, and grasping for holdings with our bare hands in the dark. Just half an hour into it, lovely Janina had a panic attack. Breathless and shaking like a leaf, we sat her down on a rock so she could steady her nerves. But it just wasn't happening. She was filled with not just visible dread but also hidden guilt that if she didn't continue, we would all have to turn around. So I decided to share with her what I had learnt less than two years earlier. And there on the mountain, about 3500m above the sea, I taught Janina Mindfulness. I gently instructed her to place one hand on her belly as I held the other one, crouched down so that my eyes could meet hers. I told her to feel her belly as she breathed in and out. To ignore any thoughts about carrying on or not, about letting anyone down. There on the mountain at 3am in total darkness I taught this young woman how to send her attention to her boot-clad, quivering feet and notice. Notice the quiver, notice the shingle, the cold. Then come back to her belly. Then back to her feet. And back to her breath. I'm not sure how long we 'sat' with her unease, her discomfort, maybe ten minutes? But what I do know, is that she found her breath, her feet and the steadiness to go on, for herself. There, on Jbel Toubkal, I found a gift, a purpose. I had not just helped myself get off the kitchen floor, but helped Janina get off the mountain floor, so that she could carry one and enjoy life. As Janina had no headtorch, just her phone torch, I gave her mine and used my phone instead, reducing my climbing hands to one, as the other held a small beam to light one step at a time. To be honest I was pretty scared too, but Janina's need for support gave me strength. I checked in with her from time to time but she seemed fine. Calm. Stronger, like the mountain we were climbing.

We climbed and climbed and slipped and slided our way to the summit just before the sun rose. The temperature dropped as we crowned the last slope and our head scarves and woolly hats came out. I can't remember what I was expecting but it wasn't the pyramid of metal that greeted us. Nevertheless, the view from on top of the world was breath-taking; unrestricted views in every direction, from the Marrakesh Plain to the High Atlas in the north and as far south as the Anti-Atlas and the Sahara. Like no other sunrise I had ever seen. The mountain by our feet was black and in the distance we could see the Atlas Mountains stretching out before us, below a sky that was still dark blue above our heads, gradually getting lighter, until a horizontal line of bright, white light separated from more grey sky in the valleys between the peaks. Janina, Sinan and I hugged with joy and camaraderie – we'd made it. After eight hours of fairly rigorous exercise and soul-searching bravery, much of it blind in the darkness, we made it. I made it.

I was on top of the world and quietly high
on life. But the adventure didn't end there.

After hanging out on the small summit for just under an hour, watching the sunrise in temperatures of about 4 degrees in nothing but a fleece, taking it all in, noticing our smallness in the grand scheme of things, we started the descent. Whereas the dark climb had deprived us of a visible path, and therefore hidden the reality of the sheer face we were braving, the daylight guided our way but failed to conceal the steepness of the slopes that were now disappearing under our feet. Each step we took ended in a slide, a grasp and a re-steadying, almost until we were all the way back at the refuge. As the walkers among you will know, going downhill is a killer for the knees, and while I am fit uphill (my friends say I am like am mountain goat), coming down I feel my five decades in my knees. As we caught a glimpse of the roofs of the refuge, I sighed and almost sped up a little, keen to be on flat, unmoving ground.

We didn't stop for long. A second more substantial breakfast of eggs and non-pork sausages provided us with fuel for the last three to four hours back down to Imlil. But again, shortly after we set off, poor Janina was struck once more; this time by altitude sickness. The nausea and fear of bodily releases was much greater than any guilt for slowing us down. Her fatigue was clearly visible on her pale, sweaty brow. Half way down we passed a cluster of shops and dwellings where a goat had just been slaughtered, and its many cut up parts spread out on the concrete shop front to dry. Luckily, there was a toilet shack there, for it was more than her poor stomach could stand (to be honest Sinan and I weren't thrilled either). I can't think of anything worse than feeling like you are going to vomit and poo while stranded on a mountain in a shack next to a dissected goat. Then things got worse. The sole on one of her boots came away, flapping with every step. Without hesitation, I pulled out my first aid kit and used the surgical tape to bind the shoe together and make it last the trip. So, with a wobbly tum and a dodgy boot, Janina inched her way down the mountain, reassured by me and Sinan along the way. At the pace we slowed to, I wasn't sure we'd make it for hours. We were being overtaken by surprisingly fast mules and agile children at every bend until Janina could take it no longer, so at the next opportunity our guide hailed one down and negotiated the cost of a ride for her down to Imlil. Although it was less exhausting, you could see that each rise and fall of the mule's rump brought with it a wave of discomfort, poor thing. All the way down I tried to exude compassion and dispel any concerns she voiced about spoiling our descent and maybe it worked, because she made it without needing medical attention for her altitude sickness. While Janina returned to the lodge to recover, Sinan and I went with our guide to a restaurant in the village, sat on the floor on kilims, and tucked into some western style lunch – funny how when you are physically drained, your stomach craves something it knows! And after a long shower, I met Sinan on our roof top terrace for a final tagine, looking at the best view in the world, Jbel Toubkal; the mountain that made me feel high; high on the knowledge that I have the skills, the gift to heal. I had gone to the top of the mountain to feel alive, to enjoy life, and had come back down knowing I can help others feel alive too. Whilst I had felt tiny at the top of the world, I had come back down feeling pretty mighty.

So if you are doubting your gifts or feeling small, sit still and ask your soul what's missing? What does it want you to do, to reconnect with yourself and tap into your true purpose? You might not find out on your first adventure, but I guarantee your love of life and confidence will be boosted until you do.

Step 11. Get still – see what gets stirred in your heart.

After the activity of the week in Morocco, life continued to be full of thrills. I had a week in Paris with the kids watching my beautiful, brave, youngest perform on stage and dance in the Parade at Disneyland with her theatre group, bursting with pride. I was dragged onto hideous rides that dropped me from a great height and hurled me forwards at vast speed. Then we had three wonderful, slow paced days in Paris, walking by the Seine with its relatively new sandy beaches, circumnavigating the Isles on a Bateau Mouche, and sitting for hours on the steps of Montmartre, watching a fabulous mime artist, who had us in fits of joyous laughter. Paris was followed by three glorious weeks in the Algarve among family and friends. Here again the fun continued; we raced on the wake of a speed boat, holding for dear life to the inflatable banana, being flung into cold water; we twirled and whirled down water slides; and raced each other in 200cc go karts, as had become the tradition since my son's 5th birthday. All balanced with daily sunset-gazing at our favourite beach.

Our abundance of fun was enabled by an abundance of Mindfulness teaching jobs in the Autumn term, so I treated the kids to a budget Christmas trip to New York! Christmas has always, always been hard for me; there were just three of us in the UK for my entire childhood, my family all residing in Portugal, and for the last fifteen years my brother and I had been living at opposite ends of the globe. So, this year we celebrated my youngest's 10th Birthday on boxing day and then were straight onto a plane to New York, via a quick stop in Chicago (not the most direct route, I know, but the cheapest), where we hooked up with my amazing, crazy friend Diane. The trip had been slightly jaded the day before we departed, when my father in law had criticised me for spending the money. He had even gone to the trouble of calculating what flights and accommodation would cost. I was deeply hurt when the email arrived. At the age of 46, having helped his son invest in properties for 20 years, which had grown in capital 12 times times over, I felt it was unjust to question my decisions, especially since I was funding the trip entirely by myself. Sadly, despite two years of mindful meditation, that feeling hung over me for the entire trip. Today, I am able to brush such comments aside, as I have learnt not to need to justify my actions to anyone, knowing in my heart I deserve everything the Universe brings me. And he was been incredibly generous on other occasions, so I have forgiven and hold nothing but love in my heart for him.

Anyway the children didn't pick up on my heavy heart, but they did pick up a bug. So all four of us at some point over the week in NY had to have bed rest due to sneezes, fever, nausea or body aches! Nevertheless, I was able to feel and share wonderful moments that made memories for us all. We ate Pizza in Time Square then visited Ground Zero and they were able to connect with a day that had shaped the world they had been born into. The moment the planes went into the towers I was on a treadmill in Buenos Aires. 8 months pregnant, watching BBC World news live. So for me too it was a way to revive the compassion for the people whose lives were devastated in the city we were visiting. We ate in diners, and inched our way in crowds through the rooms of the MOMA, stopping at each window to watch the snowy world outside. We visited Shake Shacks and crossed Central Park in no hurry at all, goofing on the boulders, feeding the squirrels and taking in the Winter sunset over Downtown Manhattan. We strolled along a very chilly Brooklyn park taking in the views of Manhattan and chatted with jovial NYPD officers beside a bustling Rockerfeller Centre, watching the Christmas lights and gigantic Christmas tree in awe like toddlers. We were soon like locals on the subway, easily getting around from our very basic (and economic) apartment in Brooklyn. We spent time people-watching at Grand Central Station, then recalled Mr Popper's Penguins at the Guggenheim. After an unfortunately dull New Year's Eve, where I was struck down hard and fast by a fever and shakes, leading to us spending midnight ironically watching the film New Year's Eve, set in NY from our beds, the universe blessed us with the most beautiful New Year's Day ever. The sky was bright blue as we looked down over the amazing city from the 102nd floor of the Empire State Building. The sense of calm and new beginnings was all around, as we walked aimlessly through Chelsea and along the High Line, with its serene gardens and benches to just sit and contemplate our deep sense of togetherness and happiness. Our penultimate day was a little less sunny and having sold our tickets for a trip to the Statue of Liberty, we took advantage of the grey skies to sit on the Circle Line ferry circumnavigating Manhattan in quiet reflection, listening to the history and seeing the city from a different perspective, with beginner's eyes. The Sony Innovation Centre provided pre-dinner thrills, as we donned VR goggles and allowed our senses to be stunned by sea life, as we sank into the depths, where Great Whites met us and sent us screaming off our seats into the air. We lent into the joy there, as Brene Brown says. Not worried that our trip was coming to an end. Simply enjoying each fairly unplanned day (again, the new me going with the flow). The children were almost as thrilled by our cab being stopped and searched by a Cop with an Alsatian, as we entered Wall Street to have dinner with friends from Uni. It was like being on TV! And on our last day we devoured delicious Dim Sum in Chinatown and ended the marvellous family holiday in true NY style; clothes shopping in Soho.

As I look back at the photos of that amazing trip, my heart is filled with love and warmth. My cheeks have softened and there is a smile on my face as I type. No regrets about money spent. Just an abundance of adventure, family fun, love, memories and happiness. The intensity of being in each other's company for eight days from the moment we woke until the moment we slept had been nourishing; we were creating bonds to last a lifetime. Because we deserved it.

The adventures continued into February Half Term. I had an urge to visit Cornwall, with its beaches similar to Portugal's but with no need for expensive flights. So we found a base in Trebetherik, and spent the week taking seaside walks and having movie night every night, huddled together on the sofa. By Easter however we were missing Portugal, so we set off on our first ten-day holiday in one place. We ate on the patio of our old house, visited all of our favourite beaches, and caught up with friends and family. No itinerary. Just great times catching up with places and people dear to our hearts.

However heart-warming these trips had been, the half dozen adventures had provided a constant sense of being in motion. By May 2017 it was time to stop, to be still. It was time to take a retreat, a silent one at that. The thought of spending multiple days in silence sends a lot of people into panic. To be honest, before I did my first day in silence during the MBSR course, I was horrified too. As someone who is self-employed and spends a fair amount of time working alone, I saw events with others as an opportunity to connect, to make new friendships, to hear new ideas and be energised by others' experiences. Not to sit in silence and get to know ME better. I already know me, right? Wrong!

There are certain criteria for being a bona fide Mindfulness teacher, and one of them is to go on silent retreat every year. Half of me was glad to get away, curious to experience new things for a few days. The other half of me had a huge sense of achievement that this final milestone would concretise my status as having gone from mindless mess to Mindfulness meister in just three years. I could now proudly say I met all the expectations of my new, hugely purposeful and rewarding vocation;

1. Personal participation with a Mindfulness course – check. My life-changing 8 weeks with Tessa in 2014 had led to so much more than expected.

2. Completion of rigorous teacher training – check. My two intense weeks with Patrizia and Helen gave me personal growth, great grounding ... and two lovely new friends.

3. A relevant qualification or equivalent experience – check. My Masters in Human Resource management, my Primary School PGCE and my experience in Management Development provided me with all the above and more.

4. Knowledge of the populations that will be taught – check. Books about psychology help but having been depressed myself, I had first-hand experience of that 'population'.

5. Knowledge of relevant psychological processes – check. All of the above plus a shelf of relevant books, most of them read, provided me with this.

6. Daily practice – check. Sometimes 3 lots of 10 minutes, sometimes 30 minutes in one go. But daily stopping to pay attention, on purpose, in the present moment, non-judgementally, and noticing what arose.

7. Engagement in processes which develop teaching: ongoing contacts and regular supervision – check. My monthly

supervision with Helen satisfied personal and professional needs. And I got to hear her lovely German accent.

8.   Commitment to ongoing development – check. My participation in (and now presentations at) annual conferences and the fabulous series of workshops at the Oxford Mindfulness Centre, allowed me to grow continuously … and enjoyably.

9. Adherence to the ethical framework - check.

10. Participation in annual residential teacher-led Mindfulness meditation retreats - my next, final step. Gaia House.

So, back to Getting Still. Even before setting off for the retreat, just sitting still and taking in the two-and-a-half-year journey I had been on, gave me a sense of calm and pride. A smile crept on my face and a gentle, slow sigh followed. Off I went to Newton Abbot in the 'Crystal Valley' on a sunny, long weekend in May. Gaia House is a meditation retreat centre which holds silent meditation retreats in the Buddhist tradition all year around for inexperienced and experienced meditators (more recently online too), and at that point I was somewhere in between those and wanting more.

Today when people ask me what I do, I say I teach Mindfulness and meditation. Mindfulness is the end goal, but meditation is the main vehicle. Buddhist insight meditation (or Vipassana, i.e. 'seeing deeply or clearly') teachers might explain that it is about calming the mind, so that you can get to understand your experience and yourself and thus gain the wisdom and compassion to liberate your heart from pain or suffering. Mindfulness teaching tries to explain that while a sense of calm is often a great side effect of meditation, it isn't the primary goal; we are trying to notice where our attention is, and if we find it is somewhere unhelpful, to acknowledge that, breathe into that, and use awareness of the body to come back to this moment. There is, in my opinion, a slight difference. But both complement each other. Both help us understand what makes us feel unsatisfied and how to deal with that. But Gaia House, true to its Buddhist heart, tries to help retreat goers embrace the Buddha's Four Noble truths of; knowing your suffering fully, letting go of the craving that causes your suffering; experiencing the end of that craving and pursuing a way of life that cultivates the Eightfold Path. In that sense, the retreats go further than just teaching us how to respond effectively to the difficult emotions and painful feelings that life presents us with. Gaia House aims to help those who attend to become free from subtle but widespread obsession that "things aren't quite right", so that we can all reach our full potential of peace and compassion. It offers anyone who takes part a chance to uproot their misperceptions about life, so that they can be content and connected with others. And in my case that was exactly what I got.

Gaia House is set in a stunning historic location, in the heart of the countryside in peaceful and beautiful South Devon, surrounded by hills topped with pretty copses and fields filled with cows. There you can literally hide away from the rest of the world as you explore the teachings of the Buddha and are guided by a variety of experienced Dharma teachers from all over the world. You are pretty much shut off from the physical world, but your mind is opened to the infinite possibilities of a spiritual one.

Now I have to be honest, when I chose my retreat I barely read the description of that retreat's theme; I was driven by a date that suited my busy schedule as a single working mum of three, who shares her children at weekends with her future ex. So I looked at my diary and May 26th it was, beginning of the Summer Half Term holidays. Perfect. As usual I booked the train ticket last minute, so was shocked to find that there was standing space only for the first half of the journey. Apparently Devon was a popular destination at half term for people in their late teens and early twenties, who filled the carriages, as well as the corridors and all other spaces. So, I put my bag down in the aisle and used that as a chair, no one seemed to mind. I felt quite the traveller, just like in Morocco. Youthful and carefree. Peaceful. Just accepting whatever arose. And the retreat hadn't even started!

The hours passed quickly as I stared out of the window and watched the beautiful countryside whizz past. Earlier conversations with a lift-share message board chat group on the Gaia House website, had allowed me to pre-arrange a shared taxi ride with other retreat goers, so when I arrived at Newton Abbot early, I found a small grassy green opposite the station and lay down to sunbathe until my companions' train arrived, from I knew not where. My body and mind were quite happy to do nothing other than lie, stare at the blue sky, and wait, patiently. Getting into a taxi with 2 complete strangers felt just as easy, and the 10-minute journey was filled with relaxed pleasantries as we got to know some of the people we would be spending the next 3 days with.

Arriving at Gaia House, I could sense the calm instantly. The slightly austere cubic house stood behind a lush, inviting lawn. We were greeted by gentle, friendly smiles ... and tea and biscuits. Perfect. Until then I hadn't known which chores I would be given (gardening, food prep or housecleaning) nor whether I was sharing a room or whether my request for a single room would be accommodated. I was relieved to get food preparation duties ... and my own room! At the top of two flights of airy stairs, it was small, simple and with a great view. Then we were invited to wander to the lawn and chat until everyone had arrived, sipping tea and munching cake. Chat! On a silent retreat! What a surprise. There were people of all ages, almost as many men as women, and they all looked 'normal'! Some had been before, and for others like me it was their first visit. So far so good.

We were told that silence would start at 6pm with a silent light dinner of soup, after which we would meet our Dharma teacher for meditation and an explanation of the days' schedules. At first it was a little odd to weave in and out of people to pick up a bowl and spoon in silence, to queue for the soup in silence, and to sit and eat in silence. You have a choice of staying present and mindfully enjoying your food, or letting your thoughts run wild and chat to yourself. I was surprised to notice how the mindful presence came so naturally. It was a relief not to think, just to be.

The meditation room is at the end of a sloping corridor. We all arrived in dribs and drabs, leaving our shoes outside and finding a meditation cushion in the large, long orange room. Uncharacteristically the cushions were laid in a semi-circle facing two cushions on the left side, rather than in neat rows all facing the end, as in the picture on the site. We soon learnt that this was because the retreat would be a little different and would involve enquiry. Discussion. Talking! A bit of me was disappointed, as I really wanted to prove to myself (and others!)

that I could keep my mouth shut for 3 days. But I remained curious and open-minded. Our Dharma teachers for the 3 days were Danish Suvaco Hansen and Kamalamani (Emma Palmer). Suvaco had been a Buddhist Monk but left the forests to become a psychotherapist and Tai Qi teacher. Kamalamani had been ordained in the Triratna Buddhist Order for over ten years but had recently left and was working as a body psychotherapist and eco-psychologist. Quite a set of CVs! We sat, we centred ourselves, then Suvaco introduced the theme – the courage to care: dreaming the earth. After a brief talk he invited us to notice our dreams that night so that we could share them the next day. On hearing this I was actually a little irritated; I had been having horrid dreams of destruction and being lost, and wanted to focus on the good, not what exhausted me. I was so incensed that I was pretty close to abandoning the retreat that night. Then something in me prompted me to take a breath, to notice the aversion I was experiencing, to watch the strong urge to leave and to breathe into it. Which I did. I acknowledged it, observed it with a certain amount of curiosity and pretty soon my sense of defiance had dissipated and I was willing to play ball.

After a short meditation we went to our rooms to rest before the early start. My anger about the task had melted but when I got into bed to enjoy my pillow and some silence, I became aware of chattering coming from the room on the other side of the paper-thin walls. What the? Didn't they read the bit that said 'silent' retreat? I was so keen to get to sleep quickly, anticipating a night of tiring dreams, that I got quite riled about my noisy neighbours and my body became tight. I must have dozed off anyway, because before I knew it, my alarm was chiming. 6am. Time to meet in PJs with duvet in the meditation room as instructed, to share our dreams. I found a spot of floor and lay on my back, snug under my duvet. A few people started to share their night stories and before I knew it, in one of the silences between dream-telling, I opened my mouth and started to share that night's hideous dream; me running through long, dilapidated buildings, about 4 or 5 floors high, that were crumbling beneath my feet as I ran as fast as I could away from the disappearing floor, heart pounding. It felt so normal as the words came out, and a lot less violent than in the dream itself.

After half an hour, without any discussion into what had been shared, we sat up, practiced a short three-minute meditation then returned to our rooms to get dressed for breakfast, in silence. Afterwards came food prep duty. I was one of the last to enter the kitchen, with its stainless-steel professional counters, and was pointed towards a pile of chard. I separated the leaves and washed them in a sink full of cold water, changing the water every so often, until I had cleaned a mountain of chard, all the while feeling rather mischievous, resisting the urge to laugh, like a child playing a game to see how long they can be quiet. But as I looked around the kitchen everyone else appeared to be completely relaxed in their silent peeling and chopping – was I the only one dying to make a noise?

After a pre-lunch meditation and a silent vegetarian lunch I had helped prepare, I decided to explore the Devon countryside and go for one of the many colour-coded long walks advertised on the noticeboard. A recent trip to my medium, Nicky, had told me that I would get a flash of good news on a hill in Devon, and I was happy to engineer it. With walking boots on I made my way to what was in full view from my bedroom window;

Denby Hill. The uphill walk was welcome exercise after so much sitting and the view from the top was amazing. But no news flash arrived. Mmmm? I tried to keep an open mind, rather than allow disappointment in and continued my walk home for the evening session. This started outside as we practiced mindful walking and circled the huge dying oak in the centre of the garden (some participants actually hugged the tree). That was followed by a 'sit' in the meditation hall, and ended with an open sharing session. Here we heard how Margaret (one of my 'noisy' neighbours), was mourning the death of her nephew, whom she had raised. She spoke about her loss, her emptiness and how she practiced Mindfulness to manage them. And how talking to her roommate was helping. I was overcome by a sense of empathy and compassion, and a touch of guilt that I had wished them to be quiet the night before. That night when I went to bed, less angry at the thought of having to recall my dreams, they began to chat again. And now knowing the pain my neighbour had suffered and the relief she was getting from talking with a fellow human being, rather than feel tight at the sound of their joyful voices, it was as if I was listening to a lullaby, as I drifted off to sleep. It is amazing how feeling compassion has such a profound effect on your own body and on your experiences.

The next morning we descended once again in PJs and duvets to share more dreams. We chopped more veggies (still resisting the urge to laugh) and we meditated in strong silence. I tried a different route for my walk after lunch, across a field of rather beautiful cows and slightly less beautiful sheep. My mischief continued as I spent our reflection time on my bed writing some of my Mindfulness Shuffle 50 Activity Cards (which I am so proud to say were published six months later and have now sold over 1000 copies). The evening teaching invited us to explore 'breathing' mother earth, as we lay on her, with just a carpet and some concrete between our bodies and this thermic planet we float around in space on. My mind was constantly drawn to images of the watery part of our planet, which takes up over seventy percent of the earth's surface, and I experienced a sense of calling from the sea. I couldn't wait to get to bed to hear more bedtime stories from the room next door; I couldn't hear the words clearly, but the voices were like a mother singing to her child.

Time was flying. Our last day followed the same routine; share, chop, sit, eat, walk, meet. And in our final group discussion we ate in a large circle facing each other, with a microphone on offer, should we want to sit in the middle and share our last thoughts with the group. Having not hesitated to divulge my dreams while we all lay on our backs, eyes closed each morning, I was suddenly scared to take the mic and centre stage. But as a few others went first, my fear melted and before I knew it my hand was in the air, a mic was in it and I was walking towards the cushion in the middle of the circle. And knowing there was no judgement in the room, trusting my words would be warmly received, they just flowed. I shared that the earlier sensation of floating in the sea on mother earth had felt like sensing earth's in and out breath, as the water ebbed and flowed. Out of my mouth came the realisation that Mindfulness had given me my breath back over two years earlier, when I so desperately needed it on the kitchen floor, when all I could do was sob. And now mother earth wanted me to help others find their breath again too. I had had the courage to face my dreams, and I had found my calling; the courage to care. To heal.

What started as a prerequisite for being a Mindfulness teacher, turned out to be a three-day retreat where I would, as promised, gain deeper wisdom. Over those three days, as I battled with the instructions, I got to know my tendency to judge an experience and the urge to leave if things aren't as I expected or wanted. I learnt to enjoy stillness and silence as a way of connecting with others and to accept others' rules. The three days also enabled me to notice a slight striving to always be physically active and my need to be in nature. I came to see how I strive to manufacture situations that have been foreseen or predicted, willing them to happen NOW, showing a slight impatience to let the Universe do things in its own time. Since there had been no flash of news on the hill, that taught me patience and to let things unfold, trusting that good will come eventually. I learnt the power of compassion to alter how and what you hear. And finally, I learnt to let go of preconceived ideas about what a retreat is, and to have a beginner's mind and just sit still and see what arises, which would help me run my first two retreats so successfully. I left Gaia House ready to sign up for another, longer retreat, and took not just muddy boots back to London, but an overwhelmingly strong sense of purpose. Namaste.

If you lead a busy life and feel like you are constantly on the go, consider a retreat. It doesn't have to be a silent one. But show yourself some self-love and take time to step off the hamster wheel and be still. You won't regret it (and of course, you can join me on one of the retreats I now hold!).

*Pause for a moment. Allow the journey I have
shared with you above to sink in.
To feel it in your body. To feel the light I found
yourself, for it can be yours too.*

I went from on the kitchen floor in October 2010 and again in June 2014, to the top of a mountain in Morocco in 2016 and up a hill in Devon in 2017 (not to mention to the summit of Mount Kilimanjaro in 2020). Along the way I caught my breath and became, as the meditation is called, strong like a mountain. Strong and driven. Driven to carry on loving myself before anything else. To carry on living in this beautiful, precious moment, and determined to start living the life I desired. Me. Not we. And FOR me, not for anyone else. The next step for me, and for anyone wanting to be the best, happiest version of themselves, and to live a life of joy, peace and abundance, was to make sure I was going in the right direction. To revisit what I valued and needed to live as the true me. To review what in life brought me happiness, and where it was lacking. To look compassionately at my strengths and allow these to propel me towards my desires. To capture these desires visually so I could focus on them and make them happen. And finally, to make sure the people in my life were serving me; that I was surrounding myself with people who nourished me and with whom I could exchange the energy of abundance. My tribe.

These last 4 PRACTICAL steps are how I did just that; laid the stepping stones of my path to abundance of health, wealth and happiness. They could work for you too.

Step 12: Get the life you desire: Know your soul's values and needs

Having invested in releasing blocks and unleashing the authentic 'weird' me that had been hiding for a while, it was time to really understand what it was I desired from this life, what was missing and what I had in me that would bridge that gap.

Sometimes we need an outsider's perspective and a good old kick up the bum to get us going. I am sure my experiences are not the only way to get it, but it worked for me. I decided to start by getting recommendations from people who had had a coach. And although some of the tasks I was set by the coach I first hired were helpful, there was something about them that didn't sit well with me, so I let them go. I knew I would come back to the idea of having a coach later, but at that time my conviction was strong that I had it in me to direct myself alone. It still is. Something in me rejected the suggested starting point of looking at goals, strategies and tactics, which can be an effective and efficient way to run a business that has already defined its mission and values. I wasn't completely turned on by making sure I was speedily successful in achieving my goals. First I wanted to KNOW what goals would set me on fire, before deciding how to get there. So I read. I explored coach after coach, model after model, until I found something, or rather a combination of things, that really resonated with how my path was unfolding.

We humans are interesting creatures and I was getting to know my brand of creature better by the day. To know the half a dozen or so values my soul craved. Take certainty for example. Most people need a fair amount of certainty in their lives; they strive to know what is going to happen and if possible when. And like many others, I like to know when the next client will appear and what my cash flow is going to be like over the next 6 months. I like to know more or less that I will be able to pay the bills. For some, when this certainty is lacking they can experience anxiety. I however, have been blessed with the lion's share of being able to bear the 'unknown'. I guess this is what enabled me to leave the best paid job I have ever had back in 2003 to become a self-employed Interior Designer (I had studied design on the side during my 1st pregnancy and maternity leave.). My ability to live with uncertainty prevented any need to be in a job that involved being over-controlling or inflexible. It enabled me to trust outcomes and go with the flow, handy when your clients change their minds every two minutes. At the time I didn't question why I was so happy with uncertainty. But working for others, knowing day in day out what life would bring, felt stifling. Someone told me a few years ago to 'stick to the plan', sending shivers down my spine. For a while, a last-minute change of mind might cause momentary indecision in me. But when that quickly passes, it leaves the door open for spontaneity and unexpected, wonderful opportunities. That's what I value. What I need. What I desire. How much certainty does your soul require?

The opposite of uncertainty is a need for variety and newness. And I'm not alone. Most of us like the sensation of taking risks (especially from the age of 15 to 25). Whether they are small ones (like trying a restaurant we have never been to), or huge ones (like trekking to the top of Mount Kilimanjaro which I did in 2020 with only 3 months' notice), uncertainty gives us all a buzz. Have you ever asked yourself how important newness is to you?

I have often been criticised for always being on the go or having a new project on the go. Looking back, my wanderlust took us to South Africa and Mexico, becoming avid divers on the way. Three years after buying our first flat in Fulham, I suggested we look at moving to trendy Clerkenwell, to a modern loft apartment. So we explored amazing options in converted office blocks, with rolling walls. It was fun. And over the Millennium we packed our rucksacks and spent a month exploring Thailand and Malaysia. As luck would have it, an even bigger adventure turned up, in the shape of the move to Argentina. But it all felt amazing. So when we decided to get married before expatriating, with just a four-week engagement, again people raised their eyebrows and asked why the hurry (assuming I was pregnant)? People can be quick to judge or criticise when others break the mould. But where there's a Will(e) there's a way, and in the space of less than 3 months we had an engagement party, two wedding parties, a 4-day honeymoon, a joint 30th party and moved to Buenos Aires. Phew.

Even there we explored bold flats to rent, some requiring serious amounts of work. The risk scared neither of us. For a year we travelled as much as we could, exploring all 4 corners of Argentina – Mendoza, Jujuy, Iguacu, Ushuaia and Peninsula Valdez – despite being pregnant and while also sneaking in weddings in New York and London. Sadly, as mentioned earlier, we were back in Blighty 15 months later, but resisted settling back down in the UK by exploring a life in Lisbon. However, the then recession made that impossible, so Fulham it was, settling for revamping the flat instead. But not settling for long. A year later we were house-hunting once again. Within four months we had sold a flat and bought a 3-bed house and started a renovation. As you know, baby two came along, as did a loft extension. And a trip to Vietnam. Baby three came along. And a rear extension. Our, my, love or need for newness didn't fade, even with the added challenge of three children to raise. That bit felt good. Then a move to Portugal. Then the purchase of a house and a second renovation. Then stop. Or rather crash. End of newness … for a while.

So, knowing that the need for variety and newness had been there for nearly 20 years, I could have concluded earlier, had it not been for the unfortunate onset of low mood and depression, that it was something I valued. I needed. That it was part of me. And in a way, my unplanned journey depicted above was a way of bringing that back into my life and acknowledging it. Of coming alive again. Of being alive and knowing it. Knowing me.

Another value we know humans have, is the need to feel connected and loved. Yes, there are some people who chose to live solitary lives and claim to prefer their own company. However, in my experience this is to avoid the effort of compromising or because they are too set in their ways. Or because they are so on edge and ill at ease with something, that any activity around them becomes stressful or unbearable. They have disconnected with the loving, sociable creature they are at heart. But most of us need to be with family and friends. How important and energising is connection for you?

Even in my darker days, I naturally combined my love for newness of surroundings, with my deep value of the many amazing friendships I have. No sooner had I landed back in the UK in 2010, than I planned weekends whenever I could to visit friends around the UK; in Birmingham, Peterborough and Oxford. I invested time and money in visiting friends further afield in Dublin and Barcelona, squeezing in as many trips to see my family in Lisbon as possible. I was vaguely aware of a fire burning, driving me to book the flights, but I hadn't yet stopped to ask myself why. I wasn't totally aware of my soul's need to connect. To love.

It is also worth exploring your need to feel important and original among the other 7.8 Billion people on this beautiful planet. One of my favourite kid-movie moments is in 101

Dalmatians, when the daddy dog is trying to count his pups while, as you would expect from a parent of 101 offspring, falling asleep and Patch comes up to him and asks if he is one of a kind … We are ALL one of a kind, ALL unique, but we do still need to feel special, to feel that we have a significance during our time on this planet in this lifetime. Striving too hard to stand out can be exhausting, egocentric … and pointless. But it is important to acknowledge how much this drives us, to give ourselves permission to be conspicuous, to step out and take centre-stage. How much does your soul crave feeling important to others?

Next try to understand how important personal growth and progress are to you. All humans need to work towards self-fulfilment of some kind. Lack of progress leads to stagnation and discontentment. For some, steady progress in a career suffices. Or taking on the odd new hobby here and there. But others crave perpetual, stretching levels of self-development. Where do you sit on this one? Are you constantly at the self-help shelf, doing online courses, trying new things? New skills, new jobs? If you aren't dedicating enough time to your development you might feel low. If you dedicate too much, for example, just because others you know are, you will again feel exhausted and misaligned … it won't feel like fun. How important is growth to you and what drives you to seek more?

Finally, and perhaps most importantly, before embarking on any next step of our journey, we should ask ourselves how important it is to us to be contributing to the wellbeing of others; people, animals, the planet. Some people find this calling early on in life, and become doctors, vets, environmentalists, campaigners, lawyers, politicians. For others the urge is less palpable and we can spend decades wandering around, slightly dissatisfied, doing a little, sometimes by accident, but essentially unaware of our need to share more of ourselves with others. How important is it for you to step out of yourself, to be there for others?

When you are ready, explore each of these 6 areas, ranking them in order of importance to you. Then estimate how much of your time you dedicate to each of these values and how you do that. The results will be eye-opening. Now acknowledge what you need to change to meet your needs so you can stay motivated as you go. Which of your values are you neglecting? What in your life goes against your soul's values?

In addition, once you have value-driven goals, look at whether you are spending your time on getting them in the mid to long-term and truly recognise what drives you as you work towards them. Your WHY. Otherwise you might find yourself working towards goals that aren't aligned with your true purpose.

Step 13: Get happy; know where to focus your attention

Who hasn't tried New Year's resolutions, only to find that 3 weeks into the year, old habits have crept back, despite good intentions? The best way to ensure our 'resolutions' will stick, is to understand the role of values and purpose as above first, then visually analyse 11 areas of life, that you would like to focus on because *you* value them ... not because you feel you should because everyone else does so.

Analysing the 11 aspects of your life:

I. How happy are you with your career, business or studies? From 0 to 10 how would you rate your satisfaction in these areas? Are you in a job you love? In a role you enjoy? Studying something you are really interested in? How many of us have spent decades without stopping to ask ourselves this? As I mentioned at the beginning of this book, I walked onto a degree course suggested by my teachers that I didn't enjoy, which I then rectified as a post-grad. I then took on a role I despised just because it was the place I wanted to work at. This was soon corrected by moving to a similar organisation, where I did a Masters I loved but set aside, to pursue a job for more money. This did turn into something wonderful but that too was abandoned for the sake of experiencing working abroad, sadly again in an office I came to detest. And that was all in the space of 10 years. I could go on describing how I embarked on things just shy of my true desires for another 15 years. I have no regrets. I am lucky to have found true happiness and 'job' satisfaction at the age of 45 … but it could have come sooner. And with less work-related heart ache. So, ask yourself, how satisfied are you with your work?

II. How happy are you with your financial situation? Do you wish you were monetarily wealthier? Sometimes we avoid having a good understanding of our income and outgoings, through disinterest or fear. It is crucial to know what your profit and loss is. But that is just the practical side of financial health. The other, more taboo question is 'how much money do you wish you had?'. So often we are raised to think money is evil or unnecessary (the latter being my case). But there is nothing evil about wanting an abundance of money for a nice home, good education, ample travel and to enjoy all that life on this planet has to offer. If you were to list everything you would like to do in a month, a year, a decade, how much money would it take? How much do you want to work towards getting it? There is no need for guilt to come with monetary desires. We deserve to live life to the full. The more we have, the more we can share with those less privileged, the more we can offer our time to help others. It all goes around.

III. How happy are you with your current health and fitness level? This is less of a taboo than money, but is potentially just as riddled with emotions of guilt (which is pointless in both situations). To live a long and healthy life, could your body and mind be stronger, more energetic or more resilient? Are there things you could do (remembering to avoid the phrase 'should' do) to look after this wonderful gift you have been given? Without any consideration for what Olympic athletes or just your superfit neighbours can do physically, are there areas of your health that you would like to improve? I didn't start getting into fitness until after No.3 at the age of 37, but now almost 15 years later, can't imagine a week without a jog or at least daily yoga stretches. It is never too late to start.

IV. How happy are you with your social life? Do you wish you had more friends or spent more time with them? We all need a 'tribe' to hang out with. People we trust, who accept us without judgment. Friendships take time and effort to nurture but the reward is exponential. In this world of career competition and financial stress, do you have a balance between the time you spend investing in your career (often working for someone else's gain) and the time you invest in building and maintaining strong and FUN relationships. No man is an island. It could be a coffee, lunch, a drink, a trip to the cinema, a gallery or the theatre. A run or just a walk in the park. Poker or knitting. Is your inner social soul satisfied? If you have experienced a separation or divorce, losing friends is hard to bear, so make sure you are filling any holes that were inevitable collateral damage from the end of a relationship.

V. Which brings me to a big question: are you happy with your family situation? Having lived my whole life in a different country from my family, I have fought with maintaining long distance connections. And having had copious skeletons jump out of the closet at me, I have fought with accepting lies and deceptions. Families can be the bane or love of our lives. I don't believe blood is thicker than water. But if you have any family issue that makes you feel anything lower than a love vibration, then the dissatisfaction will infiltrate your happiness in general. Whether it is a question of more quality or more quantity time. Whether it concerns your parents, siblings, partner or children, remember to check in with how happy you are with your family situation. Don't go to sleep on an argument, as they say. But equally don't sacrifice your peace of mind around family members who undermine your happiness. You can love someone and not want to spend time with them as they are.

VI. A natural next question then is are you happy with the love and romance in your life? This is clearly an area that made me miserable for, if I'm honest, at least 4 years before we separated. And I did try to address and bring it to the table but that kind of exposure just pushed him further away. After learning to love myself, as shared with you in Part One, and finding the resilience to sit with what was difficult in Part Two, I was able to acknowledge that I had craved a knight in shining armour to look after me and love me intensely, like in the movies! And probably since my father died when I was two. Despite being a feminist and fiercely independent, I needed the reassurance that someone had my back and craved obvious demonstrations of love. So, to make sure you have the love life you desire, just ask yourself if you would like more intimacy, more time, more affection … then take responsibility for getting it, gently.

VII.   Do you have enough of the kind of fun that makes you beam with joy? That makes you bend over laughing, until your belly hurts? In this world of doing, we so often forget to 'do' fun. Once I had become single, it became obvious that this had been lacking in my life, as I immediately embarked on a festival of fun. We went bowling frequently, visited the Harry Potter Studio Tour and I bought an annual Merlin card and took the kids to Madame Tussaud's, Warwick Castle at least twice and even Alton Towers (a four-hour drive!). And as mentioned, I drove or flew to anywhere we had friends and used my kid-free time to catch up with friends at home and abroad. As a couple, my zest for life and quest for fun had been slightly quashed by a cautious and prudent partner, but once single, my fun-seeking soul was unleashed and limitless. So ask yourself, what you would do differently to have more fun if time and money were no barrier, so that you can re-prioritise and set about doing it in a way that is affordable.

VIII.   Are you happy with what you are contributing to your local and global community? You might not know this, but acts of kindness and gratitude release happy hormones in us. And so charity, however small, even just saying a thank you, is as good for your happiness as for the recipient of your kindness. As soon as I had been able to get out of survival mode and into a place of self-love and presence, I found a new level of compassion and desire to contribute, that I hadn't been able to tap into beforehand. Using my skills as a facilitator, I was soon able to channel this desire into being a volunteer coach of Parentgym's 6-week parenting programme at local state-maintained schools and now run near-free Mindfulness 8-week courses for my local Alzheimer's Society dementia hub. Neither of these would have been possible if I hadn't softened first, then focussed on what my heart desired –

service. It can be as little as a monthly subscription to a worthy cause, chatting to the elderly, offering your amazing skills you've identified above for free, or starting your own charity. If you feel a desire to contribute more, ask the Universe to present you with a way, as it will bring you immeasurable happiness, joy and peace.

IX. Are you happy with the efforts you are making to grow personally? Grow or die, some say. Maslow's hierarchy of needs (1943) explains how our motivation decreases as our basic needs are met, first our physiological ones (food, water, warmth, sleep) then our need for safety (a home, work, money – where many of us will have dropped to in the recent days of Coronavirus concerns). Once we have those, we can stay motivated and at high vibrations, only if our psychological needs are met; namely for love and belonging (be it with a partner, family or friends) and then esteem (a sense of achievement and respect). Once these 4 needs are met, happiness, joy and peace come from reaching the top of the hierarchy – personal growth. Only once we are achieving our full potential and creative purpose, can we feel fulfilled, knowing we are leading the life we desire while fulfilling our purpose. So, assuming your basic needs are being met, looking at how your social, esteem and fulfilment desires are, will help you know where to focus your time and attention.

X. Are you happy with your self-image? Whether that is the way you look or the aura you carry. When you look in the mirror and say I am whole, perfect and complete, do you actually believe it? When you walk around, do you stand tall and proud as a peacock? When you walk into a room of strangers, are you happy with who you are? Whether it is physical or metaphysical, are you happy with the image you project to yourself and others? Again, when we have experienced pain, such as losing a loved one or our jobs, it is easy to blame our image and undervalue our outer and inner beauty, so take the time to ask yourself if you can improve your confidence in this area.

XI. Finally, and possibly most importantly, are you happy with your spirituality? This word often leads people to conjure up images of a hippy lifestyle living in a commune, eating vegan food and wearing tie-dye clothes. But our spirituality is actually more about achieving a balance between the time and effort we dedicate to physical and material things, and to the connection we have with our place in this Universe and to our spirit, our soul. Many people are able to satisfy their spiritual needs by adhering to a religious faith. But you don't have to be religious to be in tune with and nourish your spirituality. As you know, personally for me, as shared above, experiencing rituals and cleansings, and exploring astrology and mediumship, opened up avenues for me to develop my connection with my spirit, my soul and the Universe we exist in. However you chose to connect, start by asking yourself if you are energised with the sense of connection you currently have?

By exploring these areas mindfully and defining them with a

score of 0-10 to see where you are (0 being miserable and 10 being overjoyed), it will help you focus your attention, always kindly and with trust and patience, on the areas where you are lacking fulfilment, one at a time. I find it helpful to revisit this every 6 months – that way you can pick up on shifts as your desires become clearer, and be grateful for the changes you have enabled. Remember to congratulate yourself on your path to the life you desire.

Step 14: Get joyful: acknowledge what you are really good at and celebrate that

Let the work you have done above fuel you, energise you. Don't let that energy go until you have created an 'action plan' of how to make that vision a reality. The plan will help you capture specific goals, tactics and actions to ensure you achieve your desired, dream life. However, at this point you might start feeling sick in the stomach; the potentially long list of steps and how much they will take you out of your old self and into an uncomfortable zone, might overwhelm. Breathe, stay grounded. One step at a time.

To help you stay grounded get excited about the first step, think of the last time you were doing something passionately and totally lost sense of time due to being so totally engrossed in what you were doing? Allow yourself time to see it clearly with your mind's eye. Let yourself re-feel that felt sensation of learning something new rapidly. Where did you feel it? Find the feeling in your body. Let it spread out all over your body. See your old self performing at that high level again, relentless and untiring. Driven and happy. Ready to take action now.

To be able to carry out the action plan with ease, you will also need to know and use your strengths. Using your natural abilities will ensure you feel 'flow' on your path and reduce the sense of struggle, as each step will feel organic and empowering. You will literally 'melt' out of one step into the next, almost effortlessly, fully engaged and full or energy. None of the strengths below are mutually exclusive, but you will tend to lean naturally in one direction or the other.

So what are your personal strengths? This will need you to be honest – don't over inflate your abilities and don't deny your skills. This is about you, for you. And remember that it is counterproductive to judge yourself here. We all have strengths and weaknesses. Be kind to yourself. We are all unique and magnificent.

Start by asking yourself whether you consider yourself to be cautious (this is not a disadvantage!). Do you prefer to listen to others rather than talk? Do you have few close friends you like to spend 1:1 time with. This probably means you are strong at having good judgment, a careful reflector and good at solving problems. Or, like me, are you outgoing? Do you enjoy being in large groups, and living a gregarious, extrovert and impulsive life? This probably means you are strong at thinking on your feet, being assertive and making decisions on the spot.

There is no right or wrong, just strong.

Next ask yourself if you are particularly caring? Do you like to help others (again, like me) but are unsettled by conflict and avoid disharmony (this doesn't mean you don't stand your ground when you have to). It is likely that you are strong at being sensitive to others' needs and consider the impact on others in what you do. Or are you analytical, allowing yourself to be ruled by your head rather than your heart and sceptical? If so, you probably have a strength in dealing logically with data and don't let yourself be swayed by emotions.

Another strength worth exploring is conscientiousness. Do you have high levels of self-control and act diligently, slowly and cautiously, planning things well in advance (if so prepare to be kind to yourself if you start to feel guilty about incomplete tasks)? Or are you adaptable, resourceful, able to multi-task comfortably and enjoy moving into action planning as you go (this is like looking in a mirror for me). If so, you know you can tolerate time pressures (or the occasional burning platform!).

Furthermore, ask yourself if you are determined? Taking pleasure in persevering with hard work, tackling obstacles to complete tasks, even if it means not being a perfectionist? If so, don't beat yourself up about the imperfections and instead be proud of your intrinsic motivation. Or, on the other hand, are you more of a co-operative type? Seeking consensus and support, disliking competition? This is OK too, as it means you are good at finding a compromise and praising others.

Now think about how you generate ideas. Are you a helicopter, who prefers to see the whole picture from above before narrowing down to the best solution, seeing patterns in complex situations? Beware not to hurt others if you think something is superficial. Or like me are you creative? Bursting with ideas, some (but maybe not all) of them original, ingenious, novel ways to do things? Remember to test a few to make sure they are productive or at least aligned with your values, purpose and personal vision.

The next three I heavily recommend exploring for the sake of making your dreams come true as smoothly and quickly as the Universe allows. Ask yourself if you are goal oriented? I have nothing against going with the flow as you've read, but if you want to get off the floor, and find happiness, joy and peace, you need to take action. To a certain extent, how much you crave achievement, how long it takes for your energy levels to increase and what hours you are able to invest, will depend on the blow you have been dealt and the strength you have at any given time. But act. Draw up specific goals, starting with happiness, and ACT. Beware of becoming impatient with delays or restless if you have idle moments. Sit, trust, accept as you work towards your goals with action. And if you 'fail', let it go. Start again with a beginner's curious mind.

To achieve your goals (happiness, joy, peace, health, wealth, self-fulfilment) you will need to have a little of an organiser in you. Plan a little, keep targets in sight, make sure your work space is decluttered and tidy and build some upbeat routines into your life. In other words, set yourself up for success. You don't need to be a neat freak or become rigid and obsessed with deadlines. But make sure you have things in place to prevent slipping away from your dreams and desires, from being the best version of you possible, for YOU.

And finally be a leader. If not at your 'job', at least of the path to your dreams and desires. Lead the efforts of your inner team. In moments of doubt, remind yourself persuasively of why you are working towards this intuitive dream for a happy, true you. If others challenge you, say you are crazy (which I have often been told), stick up for yourself. But avoid being aggressive or confrontational; they might just be jealous of your courage and you might be able to encourage them to explore their true dreams too. If you are a natural leader you might try to argue with others logically, so beware not to forget that your instinct, not logic, has led you here and the Universe is waiting for you to show up and keep showing up.

Of all these areas, which are your top 2 or 3 super-powers? Set an intention to use these and often to your advantage, as you work on your happiness goal of the life you desire.

Step 15: Get peace: surround yourself with a tribe that supports your new state

So, things have come full circle. My journey started with a single step towards the bookshelf in my friend's house in the summer of 2014. I found Ruby then I found myself. The rest, as they say, is history. So surely now I can sit back and get on with the rest of my life? NOOOOOOO!!!!

When you've found out how to get from a to b, grab that map and keep on following it from b to c to d to … infinity. We are infinite beings with infinite journeys to take and infinite things to discover. It was with this in mind, that my growth-junky spirit discovered yet another growth guru and her Badass books. One of my Mindfulness students suggested it. That in itself has been key to my growth – letting my students guide me in a circle of mutual growth! When we think we know it all, we close off so many doors to new discoveries. Let the Yoda be the Paduan. Stay humble!

Reading Jen Sincero's book was like looking in a mirror and finally seeing me. Like drinking a cup of cocoa. Each sip was a creamy, sweet blanket, reassuring me that

1. I am not the only nut job out there, adamant about life and living, and helping others to want to live too

2. I am not alone in my desire to combine my knowledge about the big old Universe and little old me, in order to do justice to my few years on this rotating ball

3. There are people like me out there, who will find energy and belief in the pages of a book about someone else's path to happiness and 'success'.

Each chapter re-affirmed what I had come to learn; we all have the potential to kick butt and we all owe it to ourselves to stop doubting and start, well, kicking butt. Reading it was like watching my pebble sink deeper.

Let me explain. One of the meditations we teach on MBCT is called the Pebble meditation. It comes in the last session of the eight-week course. It is so simple, yet so powerful. Imagine you are sitting by the side of a lake with a pebble in your hand. Think about what you value, what is important to you. Let the pebble fall out of your hand and say it to yourself as you watch the pebble slowly sink deeper. Without striving, your awareness might shift. You might have a deeper understanding. So ask yourself again, what do you value? What is important to you?

Say it to yourself as you watch the pebble slowly sink deeper. As the pebble drops, your awareness rises again. You become truly conscious of what you value and what is important to you. As the pebble sinks into darker depths, your clarity rises to the surface. You can't help but look up and see the rays of light cut through to you.

In 2010 my first thought might have been "I value my family, being together is important to me". That totally drove my actions and words towards the father of my children, when he declared he would live 1300 miles away from us indefinitely. Every word that came out was bitter and every action hard. I wasn't able to sit still and watch the pebble drop. I was too hurt and angry that my dreams of an intense family life were being torn apart. I couldn't see the light.

Today, every time I guide my students in the pebble meditation, I am amazed at what reveals itself. Now as I sit by the lake and let the pebble roll out of the palm of my hand, gently breaking through the still surface creating small rippling circles, I might say to myself "I value my dreams, fulfilling my purpose is important to me". My cheeks soften. My confidence rises and my shoulders drop, just like the pebble. "I value those who lift me up. Being with compassionate, loving people is important to me". My spine lengthens as I sit taller, my lips curve into the crescent of a subtle smile. The pebble appears to be floating down like a feather in the air, rather than like stone falling through water. "I value this moment, this breath. Being alive, loving and being loved is important to me." And although I know the deeper you go, the colder the water gets, I am filled with a sense of warmth.

In many books I have read it is like watching my pebble sink to another eye-opening level of awareness. I don't think what I value or hold as important has changed that much. But the options of what that looks like and how it can be achieved have grown exponentially. My family is still what I value most, but my family isn't limited to a partner and children. The friends I have made on my journey, the wise people I have listened to, the students who have trusted me with their happiness. They too are my family. And of course being together is important. Scientists have known for quite a while that human connection and a sense of belonging are what is important for our happiness. But I can be happy even though the people I care about are spread all over the world from Chicago, to Buenos Aires, from Sydney to Suffolk and from Serbia to Spain. Together can exist apart. And all because the more I feel like an awesome Badass, the greater those distances can become without feeling faraway. The greater my family is becoming, even though it is technically shrinking, as I let go of the relationships that no longer serve me.

So how can exploring your 'Bad-assery' be your Saving Grace? Like other gurus I have learnt from, she reminds us that we all have 'baggage' that might be festering in our subconscious, making us believe that things we dream of will always be painful or impossible. On the MBCT I teach that you can imagine your thoughts as clouds passing in the sky, or the credits of a film rolling of the screen, or even as sushi dishes on the rotating belt. Here is another imagery for how to view your 'baggage'. Imagine you are at the airport waiting for your baggage to spew out of the underground dock and land on the rubber conveyor belt, so that you can heave it onto your trolley and push it out into the world with you. Instead of looking out for battered cases with broken zips and dodgy wheels, you could check in with your limiting thoughts and let THEM pop out onto the belt. Randomly. They might be "you need rich parents to get far in life", or "only bankers make money", or "you only get rich if you really slog your guts out", or even "I wasn't supposed to be well off". These negative beliefs that lead to denial or guilt, could have been packed into your cases by your parents as you were growing up without you even knowing it (as mentioned earlier in this book). Once they are there, they crash with other cases on the belt and multiply and before you know it, you have a multi-piece set, complete with beauty case, holdall and hundred litre large case. "People will hate me if I make money" could join them, or "They will think I am a fraud if I am successful". And suddenly you are sitting in front of a conveyor belt of baggage heavier than you can imagine, all staring at you to lug it around for a lifetime. Don't go there! Thank the cases for showing up, but walk away gently. These bags, or thoughts, limit you. Get a new colourful set to pack full of uplifting, enabling and abundance-bringing beliefs and experiences. At the time I thought I was just buying a cheap and cheerful case for my trip to Morocco, but now I know why it is bright blue with white flowers on it!

In addition to knowing what is lurking in your subconscious, as I discovered in 2014 on the hill in the Alentejo and on my workshop with Nicky my medium, we can only release our butt-kicking abilities if we are aware that this rotating ball we call home, has such a special place, just 3 rocks away from the sun. Close your eyes and imagine you are lying on a beach. Feel the brightness of the sun trying to burst through the barrier of your eyelids. Feel the warmth on your skin. Notice your shoulders melting into the sand and your cheeks relaxing. That warmth, that energy is coming from the ball of fire we call the Sun, but its job isn't just to put a sexy tan on our skin. How do you feel after a relaxing day sunbathing by the sea or the pool? Energised? Full of beans? What if you knew that you can tap into that same energy just by sitting still, closing your eyes and allowing its source to fill you with high frequency vibrations. Vibrations strong enough to pick you off the floor. To get you to sign up for that trip or that course. To print new business cards, build a website, order the banner, send the emails, pick up the phone, write the book . . .

You CAN turn the energy, the power, of the Universe into your own fuel. Without Redbull. Even if you struggle to believe in the power of the Universe's source energy, in the law of attraction, you must have experienced how contagious high energy is? Imagine this; you are at a party and someone comes over to you. They whinge and whine about some small stuff they are sweating. How do you feel? Do you start jumping up and down and think 'yay, I really want to hang around with this dude?' Or do your own energy levels start to fall and small stuff you hadn't even thought about pops into your mind and now YOU start sweating about it? Now imagine you arrive at that same party feeling a bit okay but someone comes to talk to you who is full of positivity. When they walk away, you are feeling much better. It is a no-brainer; vibrations affect their surroundings. So if you are emitting high frequency vibrations in the thoughts you have and the way you move, it goes without saying that everything around you will have raised vibrations; your relationships, your finances, your health ... There is one key however; to achieve this new high energy modus operandi, you have to cut the umbilical cord, release the old you, cut loose from the worrying, the denial, the guilt. Cut the anchor and sail away with the power of source energy blowing at your sails.

And once you are at sea, open up the sails, get out the jib, fly across the oceans, like those amazing 70-foot yachts racing around the globe against the wind. Don't bay hop, hugging the shore, engine on, too scared to go out to sea. Only on the open waters can you really feel free. And beware of your ego. Your Health and Safety officer. Once your ego twigs that you are up to something, something big, it will do everything it can to sabotage your trip. As soon as the shore becomes feint in the distance, it will whisper in your ear, urging you to turn back. What are you doing? Are you mad? What were you thinking? It will never work! You will go bust. Everyone will laugh. You will get ill trying. You'll grow old alone. DON'T' LISTEN! Once you have taken that first huge step and pushed the dockside away, just keep sailing ...

That bit is hard. Your ego has had decades of practice in keeping you safe. While kicking butt is fairly new. So what can you do? How can you be your own body guard when your risk-averse ego appears? The temptation might be to clench fists, tighten everything and prepare for battle. But what if instead you did the opposite? You recognised this is just mother nature using the amygdala in your brain to keep you safe. Love mother nature for that, thank her for that. But remember you have set sail for YOU. Remind yourself how unique you are. Don't beat yourself up about faltering. Sit with the difficulty. It's too easy to get cross with ourselves and let the self-doubt creep in. If you do, all you will hear is 'told you so, I knew you'd never have the guts to really go for it' or 'who did you think you were anyway, trying to be somebody' and worst of all 'give up now and go back to what you were doing before. Sit back on the floor. It wasn't that uncomfortable'.

On MBCT we often talk about treating ourselves as we would our best friend or our children. When one of them comes to you feeling insecure and full of self-doubt, you don't tell them 'I told you so'. You don't say 'oh well I always knew greatness wasn't for you'. No! you remind them how special they are. How brave. You encourage them to do something they love, something uplifting. You insist they stop comparing themselves with others and to forgive themselves for this tiny hiccup and GET BACK ON THE HORSE. Just as you would remind your best friend or child that they are SO ready and able to kick butt, so must you find the nearest mirror and re-affirm yourself; I AM BRILLIANT, BRIGHT AND BEAUTIFUL AND I'M GOING TO KICK BUTT, JUST YOU TRY AND STOP ME! Then put the kettle on, have a cup of tea and a biscuit, grab a fluffy throw, call a friend and nurture your soul. Start again tomorrow. Odds are, you will wake up refreshed and wonder what all the fuss was about. If you are going to do this, it's non-negotiable … now where is that sledgehammer?

Last piece of advice then, is surround yourself with people who believe in you and your dreams. Who will keep your vibrations high and help you sweep doubt away when it appears. That's what true friends are for.

… Get going!

So, as you set off in pursuit of the life you desire, using some or all of the 15 steps above, remember too these key things, to ensure you stay aligned with your dreams:

- Where you choose to lay your attention, will affect your feelings, emotions and urges, so focus on things that make you feel great!
- Change doesn't happen without emotion, so let yourself really feel things!
- You have made the decision to work towards something, so stick to it!
- Have faith in you. You are amazing.
- There exists a Law of Attraction: be the best you and the rest will follow.
- You are loving and loveable.
- You are unique and magnificent.
- You have a responsibility to others to be happy.

- You have the option to be happy, joyful and at peace. Happiness is a choice.
- You are entitled to be happy.
- You can be your own Saving Grace; get up and get going. The Universe has your back, so just step forwards ...

OMG I hear you shout, but where do I start? There's so much to do, so many options. I want it all NOW!

The first time I sat down to write in 2015, I had a dutiful heart and sporadic conviction. I felt I should write to inspire others, but I didn't know where to start. Then as mentioned, my lovely writing coach, Deborah Levy, said, unsolicited, "Anna you don't always have to be responsible. Start where you like".

So for now, stop being responsible for others and just focus on

YOU. The rest will fall into place. Trust me. And START WHERE YOU LIKE. Whichever of the many steps above has resonated most with you, or whichever feels easiest now, use that as a starting point. If it doesn't change your life yet, try something else. But do SOMETHING. Sitting on the floor is NOT an option. You are worth more than that. Everything you need and want is out there, so take a breath in and GET OFF THE FLOOR.

When you are ready, find the courage in your breath to ask yourself the questions that will give you greater insight in the prologue. Then;

1. Trust in the Universe to find motivation: it's helped you find this book, so you know it is there for you
2. Don't judge; embrace others' cleansing rituals with an open mind, be willing to receive
3. Have a beginner's mind; be curious about astrology and let it guide you once in a while
4. Be patient; try CBT but know it takes time to find the right therapist, or go straight for MBCT
5. Allow for compassion; let others in or outside your faith-system show you kindness
6. Be present; Mindfulness isn't a panacea but it works for 90% of us. Breathe
7. Connect with the Universe; there are messengers out there for all of us
8. Put yourself 1st; book that trip or course, and nurture your creativity to unleash some desires
9. Accept your blocks; then destroy and let go of what stops you and manifest your dreams
10. Climb to the highest point; you'll be amazed by the you you find on the way to the top

11. Sit still; awareness comes from silence, where the strongest messages are heard
12. Look in the mirror – get to know your values and needs
13. Don't strive to fix everything all at once; pick one of the 11 areas and focus on that
14. Show yourself some self-compassion by acknowledging and celebrating your strengths
15. Create your tribe; be grateful for the people in your life who help you keep vibrations high.

Now, you are ready to be your own Saving Grace – by learning to love yourself, live in this moment and lead the life you desire.

Gratitude

Being thankful is not something I was taught as a child. That doesn't mean we were ungrateful, we just didn't get much advice about anything really. Understandable, I guess, if one parent is gone before you turn three, the other is too busy just trying to survive and pay the bills, and the rest of the family live far away … and have been instructed not to interfere. Today however gratitude is something I hold very dearly as core to who I am and to my happiness. So in true BAFTA's style, I'd like to say lots of totally heart-felt thank you's to those who were there during my often arduous journey:

- Thank you Ruby Wax for being brave and transparent in sharing your journey with the world, and for being on the right shelf at the right time. How do I want you? Just the way you are, Ruby.

- Thank you Mila and Eugenia for sharing your wise astral insights that helped explain some of the mysteries on my path.

- Thank you Jon Kabat-Zinn for creating a great programme, which has saved the lives of so many and helped me find my breath, my purpose, and now I can help others catch their breath too.

- Thank you Tessa for being such a great teacher, helping me catch 'this breath' and continuing to support me in my embryonic stages as a Mindfulness teacher (as well as recommending me to LDA who published my Mindfulness Shuffle).

- Thank you Lucy Urbanowski and Jade Ziani Di Ferranti

for reminding me how awesome I am. I think you rock too.

• Thank you Gabs and Chris Little for being my extended family and helping my desires come true in a way above and beyond any friend could imagine.

• Thank you Annabelle Pasco for the most astute sentence I've ever heard – I owe you a lifetime of Thai prawn crackers.

• Thank you Jess Simmons for walks at the beach in Greece and for traipsing South so many times for a night out; you're the best wing-woman ever.

• Thank you Fra Evrard for being you and being there, always, unconditionally.

• Thank you Pippa Furner for believing in me and bringing Jen to me.

• Thank you Nicky Huntingford for helping me trust my intuition and hear words never spoken.

• Thank you Hugh, for bringing Cornwall back into my life and for reminding me what it feels like to be falling in love and providing me with the proud realisation that I'm not willing to compromise. Intense, crazy, lasting love is still my goal. Nothing less.

• Thank you Natasha Fletcher for being the sister I never had and for making it possible for me to stay in favourite place in Polzeath so I could get this book really going!

- Thank you Nina, Oskar and Lara for being stubbornly you. For refusing to fit the mould. For showing your vulnerability. For the energy you give me day in day out. For your kindness and compassion that not all see. For putting up with me as I go around in my crazy, weird way. I love you.

- And most of all, thank you Barny for loving me and being there for almost 30 years now, even after our divorce, but most of all for leaving, so that I might find my real best friend – me.

Books that I read along the way (in surname order) that you could read after mine!:

The Journey – Brandon Bays

The Universe has your back – Gabrielle Bernstein

The power of vulnerability – Brene Brown

Into the magic shop – Dr James Doty

The Shift - Wayne Dyer

Eat pray love, and Big Magic – Elizabeth Gilbert

Into the heart of Mindfulness – Ed Halliwell

Heal Your Self – Louise Hay

Full Catastrophe Living – Jon Kabat Zinn

The work – Byron Katie

Things I don't want to write – Deborah Levy

From Battersea park to enlightenment – Isabel Losada

Dying to be me – Anita Moorjani

I am enough - Marisa Peer

You are a Badass – Jen Sincero

The power of now – Eckhart Tolle

How do you want me– Ruby Wax

Finding peace in a frantic world – Mark Williams

ABOUT THE AUTHOR

Anna is a known voice on Mindfulness in London. After two decades working in various industries, she began her journey as a Mindfulness teacher in 2015. She trained with the MiSP to teach paws.b in Primary schools and then in 2016 to teach dot.b in Secondary Schools. Shortly after she qualified as a Mindfulness Based Cognitive Therapy teacher with Dr. Patrizia Collard (author of The Little Book of Mindfulness). Finally going full circle, to make use of her earlier careers in Hotel Management, Consulting, Banking and Retail, Anna became accredited to teach Mindfulness in the Workplace with the Oxford Mindfulness Centre.

Over the last 7 years she has dedicated her work to bringing this vital life skill, centred around using your breath for stress relief, to over 6000 children and adults in schools, businesses and for the Alzheimer's Society. Having re-designed her life after 'finding' her breath, she is committed to teaching others to find theirs, so they can thrive.

Anna has been featured in You Magazine, Daily Mail, Spirit & Destiny, SW Families Magazine and the Talented Ladies Club. She has also been nominated for an Mpower National Business Award. She is a speaker at Headteacher conferences, including the Mayor of London's LondonEd 2021, and at the annual London Mindful Living Show. In December 2017 Findel LDA publishing invited her to create 'Mindfulness Shuffle – 50 fun Mindfulnessbased activities' to develop children's Emotional Intelligence, which has sold over 1000 copies.

Anna is a single mother of three teens and invests her time in championing mental health education and healing tools for everyone aged 5 to 75. These same tools enabled her to transform the devastation of separation, childhood trauma, and her mother's dementia into a force for social impact. By introducing children and adults to the powerful impact of Mindfulness as a support in everyday life, she has enabled them to increase their resilience, as well as embrace a plan B if things fall apart, as they often do.

As a carer herself, Anna teaches Mindfulness to dementia carers for Alzheimer's Society, and has raised funds for them by climbing Mount Kilimanjaro in January 2020, as well as running the 2021 Royal Parks Half Marathon. She complements her face-to-face teaching with her new online course "Live in this moment – learn to be present in just 10 weeks", and with the retreats that she runs in her beloved Algarve.

www.annawille.com

Printed in Great Britain
by Amazon